For Karrie
& Divina ——

[signature]

The World is Still Your Litter Box

by Quasi

(TYPED BY STEVE FISHER)

MORE WIT AND WISDOM FOR CATS FROM THE AUTHOR OF
THE WORLD IS YOUR LITTER BOX

ILLUSTRATIONS © 2010 BY WARD SCHUMAKER
USED WITH ARTIST'S PERMISSION

iUniverse, Inc.
New York   Bloomington

The World Is STILL Your Litter Box

iUniverse books may be ordered through booksellers or by contacting:

iUniverse
1663 Liberty Drive
Bloomington, IN 47403
www.iuniverse.com
1-800-Authors (1-800-288-4677)

ISBN: 978-1-4502-2767-4 (sc)
ISBN: 978-1-4502-2768-1 (ebk)

Printed in the United States of America

iUniverse rev. date: 04/22/2010

DEDICATION

Quasi and Steve dedicate this book, with much love, to Judy (Steve's female), to Lee Fisher (Steve's mom and a true cat nut), and to every human on Earth who has given their heart to a cat.

"If cats could drive, text and launch missiles, they would rule the world."
.... Quasi, 2010

Contents

Introduction
(For Cats Only)

Ever since the publication and smashing success of *The World Is Your Litter Box*, my ultra-hilarious how-to manual for cats, several of my fellow felines have asked me, "Hey Quasi, has the success of your book gone to your head or are you still the same humble, big white guy you always were?"

The simple answer to that question is – quite frankly – yes... the success of *Litter Box* HAS gone to my head. Just ask my human, Steve, and he'll probably tell you that I've become even more cocky, aloof, self-centered and impossible than I was before (hard to believe, but true). In other words, success has made me EVEN MORE catlike.

And oh the glory of being a world famous author! Muscular, macho male cats, who once beat me up and called me Fatso, now think I'm way cool and want to hang with me. Female cats, who used to hiss in my face when I came around, now want to hook up and have my kittens. (Actually, I no longer have my *cojones*, but don't tell them that.) Politicians, movie stars and supermodels want to cozy up and have their pictures taken with me. College professors and tweedy intellectuals want to engage me in deep, meaningful conversations about neoclassical literature and other heady matters. Endorsement requests from manufacturers of cat products are rolling in. Even dogs bow their heads in reverence when I patrol the neighborhood (well, not really).

Initially, I intended to bask in the glory of my success and enjoy my mythical status in the cat world... the proverbial retired writer in the sun if you will. But then, letters and emails from cats around the world began pouring in and convinced me to do otherwise. For you see, fellow cat, while I thought I had pretty much covered all the bases in *The World Is Your Litter Box*, the communiqués made me realize that there was far more wisdom to convey. So once again, I've put paw to paper and cranked out yet another superlative, highly-informative book that will open more doors of perception for you and help to make your life even more joyful and satisfying than it already is. Thus, you hold in your paws my brand-new literary masterpiece, *The World Is STILL Your Litter Box*, which contains deeply thought-out answers to some of the questions sent in by inquisitive cats from around the world. Questions such as:

- ❖ How can I tell if my human is a true cat nut or merely an affected *poser*?

- ❖ How can I be a more effective kitty fighting machine so I don't become "dog meat" when I go up against a larger foe?

- ❖ How can I make my human say "Awwww" no matter what act of unacceptable kitty behavior I may have committed?

❖ How can I have even MORE fun when I'm high on catnip without attracting the attention of the police or federal narcotics agents?

❖ How can I make sure my human keeps my litter box as clean as the men's room at a Shell station?

You'll find all the answers and much, much more in *The World Is STILL Your Litter Box*. And once again, all this insight is cleverly disguised as a cute cat book so your human will fork over the moolah and buy it, little realizing that it is YOU who will truly reap the benefit of its contents. HAHAHAHAHAHAHAHA!

For just a moment, though, let me pause (or, should I say... paws, har-har) and introduce myself to you poor deprived kitties who haven't read *The World Is Your Litter Box*, either because your human is a literary Luddite and hasn't heard about it, or was just too cheap to buy it for you, and reintroduce myself to those of you who read the first book but may have forgotten my biographical details.

My name is Quasi.... although Steve and many of my friends often refer to me as "Big White Guy," or simply, "Big Guy" or "Quaz." I'm part Siamese and part good 'ole boy tomcat – a curious, yet extraordinary combination of kitty attributes that allows me to be sensitive and intellectual, while at the same time, tough and unflappable... or, if the situation calls for it, a convoluted mish-mash of all of the above. I'm still at my fighting weight of 18 pounds, (or 1.28571 stone for you British kitties). As of this writing, I'm ten years old in human years, which makes me around

700 years old in Venus years, or around 6 months old in Jupiter years, depending on whether I'm feeling old and wise or young and callow.

Now I must admit... I'm a bit longer in the tooth these days, and because of the accursed pull of gravity, my tummy is little droopier and I'm perhaps a bit more jowly. But make no mistake... I'm the same dashing, crushingly handsome man-cat I always was. In fact, you might even say my ever-so-slight paunchiness gives me a kind of distinguished, statesman-like appearance. Sort of like Winston Churchill might look if Winston Churchill was a cat.

I still live in Burbank, California, with Steve and his female. Steve continues to fancy himself a writer, and because he "helped" me write my first book, he thinks he's F. Scott Fitzgerald or something. Nevertheless, we all know who has the real writing talent in THIS family. And as always, the female can't stop herself from cuddling me and kissing me whenever she is overcome by my kitty cuteness, which is pretty much whenever we're in the same room. I can't really blame her though because, after all, I am a hunk-a-hunk-a burnin' love, as Elvis so eloquently sang.

I have Steve and his female pretty well trained, but once in a while, I need to take extra measures to keep them in line. As always, Steve is very malleable and easy to manipulate, but the female sometimes requires more extensive use of my kitty wiles. Female humans come equipped with cat-like deviousness of their own, so in some instances, I have to reach back for a little something extra when going *tête-à-tête* with Steve's female. This may require such simple actions as blowing white kitty fur all over one of her black dresses, or more extreme actions such as leaving teeth marks on an expensive new pair of shoes. But I digress.

The major change in our household since my first book came out has been the addition of two new felines to our family. Yes, reinforcements have finally arrived in the form of two young brother cats named Bo Diddley and Piglet. Both have long, lustrous black fur, although Piglet's has a bit of brown and gray mixed in. Bo Diddley is a big mauler like me, although I still outweigh him by plenty. Piglet is a little squirt and was clearly the runt of the litter. Steve and his female adopted Bo Diddley and Piglet from a kitty rescue shelter. Originally, they just wanted one new cat to go along with me, but they couldn't bear to separate two brothers... so both kitties found a great new home and I have two new pals.

Bo Diddley was named after the late, great rock 'n roller, although Steve and the female usually call him B.D. or Rotundo because, well... he IS a bit on the round side. When fighting and wrestling, B.D. is the master of the four-legged defense (described later in this book). B.D. also has a beautiful lion-like ruff and keeps it very well groomed.

Piglet, on the other hand, was known at the shelter as Pigpen because – well, there's just no nice way of saying it – he's a complete mess. From the looks of him, and from his cavalier, rube-like attitude, you'd think he somehow picked up a couple of errant dog chromosomes somewhere along the way. The concept of grooming is a deep, dark mystery to Pig, as we call him. He can never quite seem to finish a lick bath, so half of him is always wet and spiky like a punk rocker from the 1970s. Pig is also a stranger to the concept of washing one's face after meals, so he often walks around with bits of Kitty Stew or whatever dangling from his muzzle. What would Miss Manners say?

When B.D. and Pig first arrived on my turf, it was a major hiss fest and whap smackdown. I hissed so much, I got a sore throat and my normally stentorian kitty voice was reduced to a hoarse, frog-like croak. But after awhile, I grew to like them quite a bit. They help me with many of the cat chores around the house, which leaves me more time to work on my effort to develop bionic opposable thumbs for cats (and nap, of course). Pig now handles the wakeup responsibilities and he's very diligent about making sure that Steve and his female never sleep past 6:00 a.m., even on holidays. B.D. is quite adept at investigation and reconnaissance, especially in closets and the depths of kitchen cabinets. And admittedly, they both have an overabundance of kitty cuteness. But let there be no misunderstanding... I STILL RULE. Put it this way... if this was heaven, I would be God and Pig and B.D. would be angels with harps. If this was Olde England, I would be the king and Pig and B.D. would be my liege. If this was the Army, I would be the general and Pig and B.D. would be grunts with rifles. If this was... well, you get the picture. Normally, Pig and B.D. show me proper respect as their superior, although sometimes, a few hisses, moans and well-placed whaps are necessary to remind them that I am *El Jefe* around here.

Naturally, it was Steve's female who came up with the idea of adopting two new cats. She made the decision shortly after we babysat two very young kittens over a weekend, and although that turned out to be a giant disaster, as you will see later in this book, she thought I could use some company. She also thought that two younger cats would chase me around and help me burn off some of my alleged fat. Harrumph! First of all, I'M NOT FAT (even though Steve and the female tried to put me on a diet, as you will also see later in this book). Secondly, cat food is much too tasty and delicious to cut back on in exchange for shedding a few extra pounds. And thirdly, if you want a skinny pet, go buy yourself a snake or an eel.

Here's just one more thing that happened in our household since the release of my first book – something which illustrates how a cat's love can conquer all...

Shortly before the arrival of Pig and B.D., Steve's mom came to visit and stayed for five days. I'm not really too up on space/time continuum constructs, so I don't really understand what Steve meant when he said that the five days felt like 500 years, but whatever... it was long enough for me to work my kitty magic.

At the time of her visit, Steve's mom was not particularly fond of cats. In fact, during phone conversations, when Steve or the female told her about one of my oh-so-cute kitty antics, she always said something like, "Oh, you and your cat! You'd think he was your child."

Actually, that's true.

Anyway, when I heard that Steve's mom was coming for a visit, I decided to take it upon myself to turn her feelings of antipathy toward cats into unquestionable, undying love. Yes, that's right... I decided to turn her into a hopeless, unabashed cat nut with no chance of salvation or redemption.

The first thing I did after Steve's mom arrived was to follow her around wherever she went. At first, she was a little perturbed, but after awhile, she started to enjoy my company and all the attention. This is one thing cats and females, mothers included, have in common... they all love it when you pay attention to them. I also snuggled up with Steve's mom while she slept, and when she sat down, I made sure to jump up in her lap and purr at 120 decibels (which is roughly the volume level of a jet engine or a Metallica concert). I kept this up for the first two days she was here, and slowly but surely, the ice began to melt.

Then, as an integral part of my scheme, I pulled a quick about-face as only a cat can.

After dinner, while everyone was sitting around watching TV, I did NOT jump up in Steve's mom's lap as she expected. Instead, I sat a few feet away, cleaned myself and acted blasé. Steve's mom patted her lap to indicate that I was welcome, but I turned up my nose, gave her a glimpse of my hindquarters and coolly sauntered away. And when she went to sleep that night, I was nowhere to be found.

Steve's mom couldn't believe I had shunned her.

"How come Quasi won't sit on my lap anymore?" she asked Steve. "And he didn't sleep with me last night."

"But mom," said Steve with a smirky grin. "I thought you didn't like cats."

"I never said I didn't like cats."

Next stop... another kitty convert.

To drive the point home and show Steve's mom how cold the world can truly be without the comfort and love of a cat, I ignored her for a couple more hours. Then, to her great relief, I cranked my kitty charm-o-meter up to full power. I purred. I nuzzled. I looked cute. I meowed coquettishly. I sat in her lap and let her pet me. At night, I snuggled with her and burrowed under the covers like a spelunker. I ask you... how can ANY human go through life without a cat?

When it came time for Steve's mom to go home, Steve gave her a hug and a kiss on the cheek.

"I'll miss you," she told Steve and the female. "But I'll REALLY miss Quasi."

And it wasn't long before Steve's mom got a cat of her own – a beautiful little calico kitty named Emily – and now when Steve calls her, all she talks about is... uh-huh, that's correct... HER CAT.

Mission accomplished.

Anyway, enough chit-chat about me and the goings-on in my life. Time to get into the real meat (yum) of this book, which will help you outfox your human at every step and elevate the quality of each of your nine lives to levels our feline ancestors could only dream of – except, of course, for cats in ancient Egypt, who were worshipped as Gods. Those kitties certainly had it made, and after you read this book, you will too.

So remember, fellow cat, you may not be able to text or drive a car, but now you have *The World Is STILL Your Litter Box...*

Viva les chats!

How to Tell if Your Human Is a True Cat Nut

Before you get too much farther along in *The World Is STILL Your Litter Box*, you must first determine the actual depth of your human's feelings for you. Do they love you like Romeo loved Juliet? Like people in Boston love the Red Sox? Like people in Wisconsin love cheese? Your ability to master (or get away with) most of the things in this book will directly correlate with the level of your human's adoration for you.

So what you want to figure out, fellow feline, is just exactly how far your human will go to accommodate you and make certain your life is as rich and satisfying as it can possibly be. In other words, you must determine whether your human is a bona fide, certifiable, true cat nut. And I'm not talking about humans who merely think cats are fun to have around and basically just go through the motions. Oh, no. I'm talking about humans who are willing to sacrifice their comfort and very way of life to make YOUR life more pleasant and enjoyable.

Here's your chance to see how your human stacks up against other proven cat nuts. Put them through these simple paces, and you will know, without a doubt, whether your human is the real deal or merely a pretender to the throne of feline fixation.

Let's start with one of the most classic ways to determine whether you've got yourself an authentic cat nut. When your human is getting ready for a good night's sleep, jump up on the bed and position yourself so that there's no possible way they can stretch out their legs or get into a comfortable sleeping position without disturbing you. Then, close your eyes, pretend to be blissfully asleep, and wait for your human to get under the covers. If they shove you aside or toss you off the bed, their devotion to you might be a bit in question. However, if they're willing to sleep with their legs splayed apart or bent at odd angles, if they're willing to contort themselves into a pretzel-like position that would make a Cirque du Soleil acrobat uncomfortable, or if they're willing to accept only six or seven inches of space on a king-sized bed, all to make sure not to disturb YOUR sleep, then your human is, without a doubt, a true cat nut.

Need more convincing? Try this one. If your human is like Steve when they come home from the grocery store, they'll generally leave at least one paper bag out for you to play with. After you have thoroughly explored the inside of the bag, smash it down and lie on it until it's perfectly molded to the contours of your kitty girth. For good measure, chew up the open end of the bag and punch holes in it with your claws so it looks REALLY ratty. Then take a nice log nap on the bag, making sure to get plenty of cat hair and kitty drool on it. If your human sees the disgusting mess (to them anyway) and throws the bag away, the extent of their cat kookiness could be suspect. However, if they leave the bag out for weeks because they know you worked so hard to get it just right, then they are, indubitably, a true cat nut.

Food is another infallible way of determining whether your human is worthy of being called a true cat nut. When your human sits down for dinner, regardless of what they're having, trot on over, plop yourself down, and stare up at them with a look that says, "Oh, please, most wonderful one... that food you're about to eat looks so tasty... can I please have just a little piece?" This will probably cause your human to say something like, "No! This is not for kitties." Just keep on staring at them. Rock back and forth slightly, and if necessary, utter a plaintive little meow or two. If your human holds fast and still refuses to give you something, their standing as a passionate pussycat lover could be on shaky ground. However, if your human caves in to your kitty cuteness and submits within seconds, then they are, unquestionably, a true cat nut. I personally never have to wait more than one minute before Steve or the female give me something off their plate, although of the two, Steve usually crumbles much faster.

Same thing with cat treats. Go to wherever the treats are kept in your household, be it a cupboard, the refrigerator – whatever – then sit there with a heartrending yet expectant look on your face. Your human might say something like, "No way. You've had 49 treats already today." Continue to sit there, staring in the direction of the treats. If your human is a true cat nut, they'll give you just one more treat (that is, until you decide you want another one).

Still not sure? Well, if your human is an extreme kitty aficionado, they'll blame themselves for any wrongdoing you might commit. Let me give you an example. The other day, Steve was trying to give me a pill which, needless to say, is not my favorite thing. In the process of resisting and putting up a good fight, I accidentally scratched one of his fingers and made it bleed. As Steve was standing at the kitchen sink running cold water over the wound, the female came over to check out the damage.

"Geez, he really laid you open," she said.

"Oh, that's okay," said Steve. "It's my fault. I was giving him a pill."

Yes, that's right... if your human is a true cat nut, you can even draw blood and get away with it!

And finally, here's the cat nut acid test. Mosey on over to the couch and check out the condition of the arm. If its totally shredded (by you), and if you are allowed to keep on shredding with nothing more than a token, halfhearted "Stop it!" from time to time, your human clearly cares more about you than the furniture, and hence, is conclusively a true cat nut. Some cat owners (including Steve and his female) are such shameless kitty fanatics, they'll "let" you keep sharpening your claws until the couch is beyond the condition where it would be accepted by the Salvation Army. At that point, they'll either reupholster the couch or buy a new one, in which case, you'll have to start the arm shredding process – dare I say it – from scratch.

Need even MORE proof, Mr. District Attorney? Ask yourself the following questions to help you determine whether your human is the unabashed cat fanatic you've always wanted. If you can answer "Yes" to more than five or six of these questions, there's a pretty good chance you've got yourself a genuine cat nut...

❖ Does your human purchase products primarily because they think you'll enjoy the boxes they come in?

❖ When moving into your current residence, did your human forsake the ideal home in a nice neighborhood simply because it lacked EXACTLY the right spot for your litter box?

❖ Does your human buy you every cat toy known to man, then allow you to leave them out all over the floor (or wherever), even when company comes over?

❖ Does your human leave their shoes out solely so you can bury your nose deep inside and take a nice long nap while enjoying the high-quality bouquet of human feet?

❖ Does your human accept the fact that as a kitty, you're going to be kacking up hairballs in all parts of the house, including on top of some of their prized possessions?

❖ Does your human refrain from taking long vacations so they don't have to be apart from you for more than two or three days at a time?

❖ Does your human let you get kitty hair on everything and have an understanding that God invented lint rollers solely to remove cat hair from clothing (and other objects)?

- ❖ Does your human allow you to sleep in the linen closet on top of clean sheets and towels, even at the height of shedding season?

- ❖ Does your human allow you to walk on the kitchen counters and investigate (or eat) whatever you might come across?

- ❖ Has your human severed diplomatic relations with all their family members and friends who are allergic to cats?

So there you have it, fellow cat...a multitude of ways to determine whether your human is a true cat nut or a second rate Johnny-Come-Lately. If you've found that your human falls a bit short of true cat nut status, don't be discouraged. Just reach deep into your bag of kitty tricks and keep hammering away. Before long, you'll find that your human, too, has succumbed to your considerable charms and now qualifies for inclusion in the pantheon of praiseworthy cat crazies.

Cat Sounds and What They Mean

Wherever I go, whether it's just to the end of the driveway or to a faraway land (in my mind, anyway), inquiring cats always ask me, "How can I make my human understand me when I speak? How can I convey my true thoughts and feelings? How can I make my demands known without having to go through a big song and dance?"

Hey, I know what you mean. Don't you just hate it when you tell your human that you want to go outside, and instead, they think you simply want a little scratch behind the ears. Or you tell your human you want some food NOW and they wrongly think you want them to brush you. Or you try and warn them about dangerous, ill-meaning poltergeists in the house and they think you want a tummy rub. I know... it's VERY frustrating.

According to scientific and anthropological studies by humans who clearly have nothing better to do, we cats are capable of producing 16 distinctive sounds – or words – to express ourselves to our humans. Considering that cats possess the wisdom of the ages and are aware of everything that is known and unknown in the entire universe, 16 words don't give us a whole lot of latitude to convey the breadth of our knowledge or demand something simple like quality lap time... especially when communication with humans can be a challenge to begin with.

But take heart, fellow orator. Each word in our vocabulary can also be used in an interrogatory manner (that means questioning for you non-attorney kitties), so this effectively expands the list – if my math is correct – to 32 words. Some thickheaded humans may have trouble determining whether you're using a particular word as a statement or a question, but if you use the proper inflection and adamantly repeat yourself if necessary, I'm sure they'll eventually get your drift.

For your knowledge, and your human's edification, here are our 16 words and the meanings for each:

"Meow"   Drop what you're doing immediately and pay attention to ME.

"Rao"   Could you please get off your lazy – beep – and feed me (edited for kittens).

"Mao"   My favorite Communist leader.

"Air"   What we breathe.

"Rare"   How I like my steak.

"Where"   What I want to know about Amelia Earhart.

"Purr-air" What I say before I lay me down to sleep at night.

"Wow"   Hubba-hubba!

"Ow"   Me imitating James Brown.

"Ankh"   Act like an ancient Egyptian and worship
           me.

"Air-row" What Robin Hood and his merry men
           shoot.

"Air-or"   When a baseball player muffs a play.

"Rah"   You won't get away with this.

"Gare"   This house is full of demons. Run for your
           life!

"Rohr"   Stand back – my inner lion is about to be
           released!

And here are the meanings of the same 16 words when
used as questions:

"Meow?"   Have you ever seen anything cuter than me?

"Rao?"   Can we watch something on TV that I want
           to watch for a change?

"Mao?"   Who put Oregano in my catnip stash?

"Air?"   Who wrote the book of love?

"Rare?"   How am I supposed to text with no opposable thumbs?

"Mare?"   Hey, I'm trying to sleep in here – could you please hold it down?

"Where?"   What have you done with my favorite paper bag?

"Purr-air?"   Could I please have my kitty water on the rocks with a twist?

"Wow?"   What's the female up to now?

"Ow?"   Could you please move your tush out of my favorite chair?

"Ankh?"   Hey, what are you doing with that kitty carrier?

"Air-row?"   How 'bout a side of fries with my Kitty Stew tonight?

"Air-or?"   Why did you invite THEM over?

"Rah?"   Just where do you think you're going at this hour, buster?

"Gare?"   You want me to do WHAT?

"Rohr?"   Was your hunting trip to the grocery store successful?

So that's it, fellow Speaker of the House – our 16 different words and what they mean, both as statements and interrogatories. I know, not exactly the vocabulary of a poet laureate, but still... if you chose your words carefully and correctly, you should have no trouble getting your point across. Just remember not to speak too quickly or run syllables together in an unintelligible mishmash as some of us kitties tend to do when we get excited or worked up. And if you come from a different country than your human, make sure you don't lapse into your native tongue when making your thoughts and demands known.

One last thing... if your human doesn't pay attention to you when you're speaking, or worse yet, if they ignore what you're saying, simply clam up and give them the silent treatment. Yes, fellow conversationalist, sometimes you must remind your human that cats are to be seen AND heard. Your silence – accompanied by a few well-timed scornful looks – will cause your human to think you're mad at them and wonder what they've done to displease you. Keep it up, and within a very short amount of time, your human will literally beg you to speak and tell them what's on your mind. Female humans have used this tactic on male humans for years, and believe me, it works!

How to Live with Multiple Cats & Alpha Males

Here's a topic numerous cats have asked me about... how do I cope with multiple cats in my household, and more importantly, how do I deal with an alpha male? Well, at the time I wrote *The World Is Your Litter Box*, I was an only cat and didn't have a lot of experience in this area. However, since the advent of Bo Diddley and Piglet, I have become (as you might expect) an expert.

The first thing to determine when you live with multiple cats is where you stand in the pecking order. Are you the big dog – pardon the expression – that no one will mess with (like me)? Are you a peace-loving middle cat like B.D., who stays above the fray and mediates battles between the other cats? Are you like Pig, the runt that gets picked on and pummeled? Or are you a cute and sassy female kitty that can do pretty much whatever you want? Be honest with yourself when determining your ranking. If you are, in fact, the alpha male, you're pretty much the king of the castle. But if you are delusional and think you're the alpha male when you're actually the low cat on the totem pole, you're probably in for some serious whapping from the real alpha.

When you live in a house with other cats, your status is sort of like the countries of the world. If you're the alpha, you're sort of a mini-version of a major superpower like the United States or China. In other words, you can do pretty much whatever you want – from invading the other cats' space to eating their food to stealing their women – without fear that anything bad will happen to you (unless, of course, one of your housemates is a dirty little squealer and rats you out to your human). Middle cats are sort of like Switzerland or Norway... pleasant, peaceful places that don't give anyone any trouble. Runts are more like banana republics that get pushed around by one force or another and are always candidates to get stomped on, squished, or shamefully humiliated in some fashion. So, once again, fellow cat, figure out what type of cat you are and where you stand in the pecking order... and be honest with yourself.

In our house, I am, without question, the alpha male. Not only am I considerably bigger than B.D. and Pig, but I'm also much tougher. In some households, the largest kitty may in fact be a "pussycat," while one of the smaller cats might be the true alpha male. But that's NOT the case in MY house. Oh, no. Here, I am the Supreme Commander, the Big Kahuna, the Grand Poobah, the Big Bopper. In our household, I rule!

Still, that doesn't mean I don't have to fend off challenges to my superiority. Being the diplomatic kitty that I am, I've established *détente* with most of the other macho males in the 'hood. However, when a new cat drifts into town, I often have to meet them in the dusty street at high noon and show 'em who's the law in these parts. This usually involves moaning, hissing and take-no-prisoners-type fighting with lots of clawing, biting, unearthly screeching and general ferociousness. It's a good thing we cats don't have opposable thumbs or there would probably be gunplay. As it is, real cat fights are not pretty, so whenever possible, I try and use diplomacy. Still, there are times when nothing but a good knockabout will get do to your point across. (For effective ways to deal with threats to your alpha maleness from pretenders to your throne, see the chapter titled "Good Fighting Techniques").

Also, in keeping with my role as the alpha male, I function as the spokescat when we kitties want something from Steve and the female, such as treats or a larger say in the running of the household. You've heard of the Commander-In-Chief? Well, in our home, I'm the DEMANDER-In-Chief.

The presence of B.D. and Pig has somewhat diluted the amount of attention I get from Steve and the female. Before B.D. and Pig arrived, Steve and the female were MINE ALL MINE. But now, alas, I have to share them, and this is one of the major problems facing cats that live in multiple cat households... how to make sure you get your fair share of attention. To do this, you must pit your kitty cuteness against the cuteness of the other kitties in the house. But how, you ask, when ALL cats are just so gosh darn cute? Well, just remember that cats are like snowflakes... even though we're all similarly blessed with extreme cuteness and stellar personalities, we're all just a little bit different. So basically, all you have to do if you feel you're not getting the right amount of attention is accentuate your individuality and trot out your favorite cute cat pose. For me, it's lying on my back with my massive tummy exposed, my paws curled like a bunny and my fangs protruding ever so slightly. Even if Steve and the female are gushing over Pig or B.D., they're powerless to resist when I lay my patented cute cat pose on them. So figure out what your best (and most effective) cute cat pose is and keep it at the ready.

Another issue in multiple cat households involves competition for chest and lap time. Fortunately, in my house, we have two laps and two chests (although the female's chest has bumps on it that sometimes make it hard to get comfortable), so the competition is not quite so ferocious. When Steve and the female watch TV, B.D. likes to sit in the female's lap, I like to sit in Steve's lap, and Pig likes to lie on Steve's legs, which are always conveniently propped on the coffee table... so everyone is relatively happy. Talk about democracy in action! Still, there are times when a cat MUST have lap or chest time and a coveted lap or chest is occupied. This is an instance when being the alpha male comes in very handy. Let's say Steve is lying on the couch reading (or nodding off) with B.D. on his desired chest. Because I'm a nice guy, I typically wait until B.D. has had a fair amount of chest time before I take action, but when I determine that he's had enough, as the old blues song goes, he's gotta move. So basically, I just jump up on the couch and muscle him out of the way with my overpowering kitty massiveness. If he objects, I'll finish the job with a little hiss and maybe a whap or two to let him know I mean business.

Now right about here, you're probably thinking, geez Quaz, all this is great, but what if one of the cats in your house mounts a challenge to your position as the alpha male?

Funny you should ask because I have that exact problem with Piglet all the time. Considering that I'm about twice Pig's size and considerably more imposing, you'd think he would automatically defer to my overwhelming majesty. But for some reason, he has delusions of grandeur or something... or maybe he's just plain crazy. Regardless, almost every morning when we're waiting for Steve to dish up our breakfast, Pig challenges my authority by staring at me – and as all cats know, staring is a MAJOR affront to an alpha's authority. Much as I try to ignore Pig and turn the other cheek like the peace-loving cat I truly am, he keeps staring until I have no choice but to strike back. This involves taking a couple menacing steps toward Pig and raising a paw to the pre-whapping position, which causes him to melt into the floor in submission. But then when I turn and walk away, darned if the little fellow won't get up and give me a whap on the hind end! Naturally, I can't let that go unpunished, so I retaliate by giving Pig a chilling I-really-mean-it-this-time moan and a flurry of whaps. This usually solves the problem, for the moment anyway.

But Piglet is a crafty little dude. More often than not, he'll challenge my authority when Steve or the female are around, because he knows they'll protect him from any serious harm. And they do, especially the female. If she sees me raise a paw against Pig, she'll immediately scoop him up and cuddle him, all the while saying something to me like, "You leave Piglet alone. He's just a little guy." Oh, please. Sometimes Steve will come to my defense and tell the female that Pig started it (if he happens to see

Pig staring at me). This doesn't cut it with the female, however, who ALWAYS sides with Pig. The little squirt could detonate a nuclear weapon in the living room and the female would cuddle him and say, "Awww... he's just a little guy."

Well, we alphas have a way of dealing with dirty rats who snitch on us. No, it doesn't involve a ride in the back of a gangster-era sedan, concrete shoes, or a call to Tony Soprano. Just wait until your human (or humans) leave the house, walk up to the squealer and say something like, "Who's gonna protect you now, punk boy?" and then administer the good thumping they so richly deserve. And if they tattle to your human, just act innocent and categorically deny everything. Hey, it works for politicians, so why shouldn't it work for alpha male cats?

Happily, living with multiple cats also has some very distinct advantages. First, you have help with the multitude of kitty tasks you're required to undertake, and you can mete out assignments based on the particular talents and skills of your housemates. For example, B.D. is an expert at looking wanton and pathetic and getting Steve and the female to give us food whenever we want it. B.D. is also a very good investigator who specializes primarily in closets and cupboards. Piglet handles the wakeup chores, and I must admit, he has developed some highly impressive techniques. If all the normal waking tricks described in *The World Is Your Litter Box* fail, Pig zeros in on any exposed skin he can find and starts licking – and licking and licking and licking – with his sandpaper tongue. This is almost as effective as a patented kitty vaccine.... otherwise known as a claw to the skin. If Steve or the female try to cover themselves completely with the blankets, Pig expertly finds the air hole (they still have to breathe), worms his way in, and licks their face until sleep becomes completely impossible. It never fails.

And, of course, both B.D. and Pig help with yard patrol and other tasks such as keeping Steve and his female from making cataclysmic mistakes around the house. If I perform an act of unacceptable kitty behavior, I can foist the blame off on B.D. or Pig (although again, Pig NEVER does anything wrong in the eyes of the female). On cold nights, we can all sleep together and share our kitty warmth. And when scary things happen around the house, such as when Steve and the female have the carpet cleaned, we can all huddle together behind the washer and pray for our lives. No atheists in fox holes.

And naturally, with multiple cats, you can have all kinds of interactive fun. Here are some highly-amusing multiple cat antics you might want to try in your homestead...

- ❖ **Roiling Cats**: When your human is dishing out your food, swarm around their legs like sharks in chum-laden water. Wander off a few paces toward your eating area, then come back and swarm some more. A few meows and little leaps only add to the fun!

- ❖ **Chasing**: Needless to say, it takes at least two cats to have a good chase. Sure, you can bolt and run around by yourself, but when you have a friend to chase, it's so much more exciting.

❖ **Wrestling**: Same thing as chasing... two cats are required, unless you're a sadomasochistic kitty that likes to beat yourself up. At our house, most wrestling matches start with a one of us administering a head cleaning to another... a nice, friendly gesture that lulls the receptor into a state of bliss and makes them ripe for pouncing.

❖ **Co-Operative Destruction**: With multiple cats, you can accomplish much more destruction in a much shorter amount of time. For example, a thorough shredding of a roll of toilet paper by one cat can take up to one hour... but with three industrious cats on the job, the work takes no more than 15 minutes. When it comes to destroying things around the house, three cats are definitely better than one.

I hope all this valuable information helps you cope with the ins and outs of living with multiple cats and alpha males. And if you're worried about sharing your human with your kitty comrades, just remember that a true cat nut will never neglect a feline member of the household. You might have to show a little patience while waiting for your doses of attention and affection (I know... patience? What's that?), but in good time, your time (and lovin') will come.

Fighting and Defensive Techniques

Got a beef with one of your kitty compadres? Are you a six-pound weakling and tired of being picked on? Not getting proper respect from punky teenage cats in the neighborhood who think they know everything? Is some macho male tomcatting around with your female, or is some Jezebel flirting with your mancat? Or are you simply a rabble-rouser who likes to mix it up from time to time?

Whatever the case may be, we cats sometimes find ourselves in situations where diplomacy fails and we are forced to take up arms (or, in our case, paws) against a fellow feline. When this happens, you must be prepared with an arsenal of good fighting techniques and defensive maneuvers, and you can't be bashful about using them at a moment's notice. This may not come easy for some of you mellow kitties, but the alternative is shameful, humiliating defeat. And let's face it... there are times when nothing satisfies like a good butt-kicking. It's the American way.

Before you raise a paw in anger (or mock anger if you're just play fighting), you must first assume the proper pose and attitude of a fighter, and this starts with looking nasty and mean. Unless you're employing some of the sneak attack-type tactics you'll learn later in this chapter, you want to let your adversary know that you won't stand no mess. So the first thing to do to is puff out your fur (not forgetting your tail), which will make you look bigger and more formidable. Then take a few purposeful steps toward your enemy, and while doing so, lay your ears back, squint your eyes like Clint Eastwood, open your mouth slightly, and emit an unearthly moan. This is the feline equivalent of when the tough guy walks into the saloon in western movies and everybody falls silent and moves out of the way. When you reach your antagonist, give them a nice loud, juicy hiss, as if to say, "Your – *beep* – is mine" (Edited for kittens).

Since Bo Diddley and Piglet came to live with us, I myself have had to mix it up from time to time, mainly to ward of challenges to my alpha maleness. Of course, being brothers, B.D. and Pig fight primarily among themselves, and I must admit, they have taught 'ole Quaz a thing or two about the fine art of pawsticuffs.

Here are some classic fighting and defensive techniques you should master and be ready to put into play at a moment's notice:

Distract and Pounce: Slowly circle the target cat for 30 seconds or so while staring unflinchingly into their eyes. Then, for no apparent reason, look toward the heavens and utter a surprised little sound as if to say, "Is that the Goodyear blimp?" When the hapless kitty falls for this oh-so-clever subterfuge and looks up to see what you're "looking" at, pounce and take them down. Dumb as this may seem, it pretty much works every time.

The Head Whap: This is a good one to use when going *mano-a-mano* with a cat of equal or slightly smaller size. Approach your adversary slowly and stealthily, or let them approach you, until you're within comfortable striking distance. Raise a paw very slowly and deliberately, all the while staring unblinkingly into your adversary's eyes. When they make any type of movement, from simple whisker motion to a pre-pounce butt wiggle, unleash a flurry of jab-like whaps to the top of their head. Make them see some stars that they won't see at the Academy Awards.

Death from Above: This is a good one for all you kitties who secretly fantasize about being a World War I ace pilot like the Red Baron. Position yourself at a high vantage point... the back of the couch, the top of the refrigerator, or if you're outside, a fence or a wall perhaps. When an unsuspecting cat walks by, yell out, "Bandits at one o'clock!" and hurl yourself down out of the sky at them. *Deutschland über alles*!

Flying Leap: Similar to Death from Above, only from a position level with your target. This technique is best done from behind when the other kitty is not looking, or is otherwise distracted.

Sure, it's cowardly and underhanded, but who ever accused us cats of being honorable?

Tummy Decoy: Lie on your back, with your back legs splayed out and your front paws curled up under your chin, exposing the entire expanse of your tummy to your intended quarry. No cat (not even me) can resist such a tempting target. When the attacker lunges in for the "kill," grab their head and do your worst. (See the next technique for specifics.)

Head Grab with Hind Leg Kick: The perfect follow-up to the tummy decoy ruse. Once you've got a good grip on your adversary's head, place the bottoms of your back feet parallel and a couple inches apart, then launch a burst of short, quick kicks at whatever part of your opponent's body is closest, which at that point is usually their belly. And while you're at it, you might want to give them a few quick nips on the chest or neck just to show them that you're no "pussycat."

The Kangaroo: Here's a technique commonly used by kittens that are still in the process of developing their coordination and fighting skills. Start with a "friendly" wrestling match that will draw your opponent close and cause them to mimic your every move in a defensive manner. Then rear up on your hind legs, and when the other kitty does the same, start punching... yes, that's right, just like a kangaroo. For three or four seconds until you both lose your balance and topple over, you can pretend you're a famous pugilist like Mike Tyson or Muhammad Ali.

Hop 'N' Bop: This is good technique if you're going after a larger cat that's lying down. In our household, Piglet often uses this one on me when I'm trying to nap, the little rotter. Sneak up on your adversary from behind, just like Robert Ford before he shot Jesse James in the back. When you get to within a few feet of the other kitty's hind end, start hopping on three legs, leaving one front paw free, and as you hop by, give them a few quick bops – or as many as you can until you pass their head. Then drop back to all fours and run for your life.

Unauthorized Butt Sniff: Here's a good one to use when you're feeling a little mischievous and want to provoke another cat into a fight. Simply stroll up to the hapless victim (again, from behind), plant your nose directly under the base of their tail, and take a good, long whiff. This will cause the sniffee to become highly embarrassed and agitated. At this point, you can do it again and provoke them into a fight, or simply chuckle and walk away, knowing that he who sniffs last sniffs best.

The Butt Bite: The perfect follow-up to an unauthorized butt sniff. Utilize the same technique used to get into a good butt-sniffing position, only this time, instead of sniffing, give the other cat a frisky little nip on the hindquarters. This will DEFINITELY get their attention and probably cause them to turn and hiss at you as if to say, "Hey, what was THAT all about?" Answer by lunging at them and taking them down.

Whirlwind of Hell: This is pretty much the only technique you'll want to use if you get into a real fight with an enemy cat, and that is to cut loose with everything you've got. This means teeth bared, claws out, loud hissing and moaning, wild whapping and swiping... the full fury of a raging kitty. You want to make sure get all your licks in quickly, because in real cat fights, the whirlwind of hell lasts only about three seconds... so you want to make those three seconds count. Needless to say, real cat fights are very dangerous and scary, so the best thing is to avoid them if you can.

Here, now, are three crucial defensive moves to use when the shoe is on the other paw and you're the one being attacked. Because all three moves require you to lie on your back, which is obviously a very vulnerable position, you must keep your reflexes taught and maintain a Defcon-4 level of readiness...

Rear Legged Defense: Here's one to use when you spot a sneak attack coming up from the rear. Flop over on your back, raise your hind legs, and use them to ward off any thrusts or lunges your antagonist might make. Your back legs are very powerful, so don't be afraid to administer few solid haymakers to the jaw to teach the creepy creeper a lesson for trying to sneak up on you.

Four Legged Defense: This is a good move to use when you want to turn the tables and go from a defensive to an offensive position in a nanosecond. Again, flop over on your back and raise your hind legs... only this time, put up only a slight bit of resistance. The idea is to allow the challenger to penetrate your back leg "defense" and lunge toward your inviting tummy. At this point, grab their head with your front paws and with your back legs, pummel their soft underbelly. A classic that pretty much works every time... even though every cat on earth is well aware of this maneuver and really shouldn't fall for it.

180-Degree Roll: Here's a good one to use if you're a bit on the round side like B.D. Lie on your back with all four legs in the air. If an assailant tries to attack from one particular side, simply roll 180-degrees to face them head on. If they move to the other side, do the same thing (only to the other side, obviously). The only minor problem with this technique is that all the rolling back and forth may make you dizzy and nauseous. If this happens, start making a gagging sound as if you're about to launch your lunch. This will cause any cat with half a functioning brain to cease their assault and back away in a hurry.

So there you go fellow combatant... a plethora of good fighting techniques to use whether you're laying down the law, making your presence felt, or merely engaging in a good 'ole cat wrestling match with a beer drinking buddy. Mix them up, keep them fresh, and you'll always have a paw up on your adversaries. And be sure not to let your defensive dexterity slide, because in the kitty world, sometimes you whap and sometimes you get whapped.

The "Awwww" Scale and How to Use It

As any cat or kitten over the age of about three days knows, no human cat lover can resist properly-administered kitty cuteness. It doesn't matter how much turmoil you may have caused, how much damage you may have inflicted, or what act of unacceptable kitty behavior you may have engaged in. One mere act of kitty cuteness will turn a true cat nut into a blubbering pile of mush and cause them to say, "Awwww," most often followed by something like, "How can one cat be so cute?" "You're the cutest kitty in the world," or "I can't stand how cute you are." In addition, "Awwww" may be drawn out to "Awwwwwww," "Awwwwwwwww," or even, "Awwwwwwwwwwww."

However, one level of cuteness might not necessarily apply to all situations. Let's say you've committed a relatively minor offense such as knocking something over. To combat your human's anger and elicit an, "Awwww, how cute," you might not have to do anything more than just look at your human with your sweet kitty face and alluring eyes. On the other hand, if you've done something relatively terrible (in your human's eyes, anyway), you might have to bump up your cuteness to a more extreme level. With all the other things going on in your harried life, you may not always have time to stop and think about what level of cuteness might be needed to placate your human and turn their anger into gushing adoration for you.

So, as a public service to all my fellow cats worldwide, I've come up with something called the "Awwww" Scale, which has ten levels that may be applied to a variety of offenses ranging from something that's just a minor irritant to your human to something that's really, really bad. For handy reference and easy use, each level of the "Awwww" Scale includes one suggested cute cat pose and an example of an offense that needs to be overcome with the cuteness associated with that particular level. Sounds complicated, but it's not. Here's how it works...

On the "Awwww" Scale (on the next two pages), simply select the level that most closely resembles your offense or act of unacceptable kitty behavior. Then merely apply the exemplar cute cat pose and wait for the appropriate response from your human. What could be easier? It's so simple, even a kitten can do it.

The "Awwww" Scale has been thoroughly tested and clinically proven to work on all cat-loving humans regardless of the circumstances and conditions. You can also use the "Awwww" Scale to merely elicit reassurance from your human that you are, in fact, the cutest kitty in the world. And you can use the "Awwww" Scale as often as you like, without any fear of failure or damage to the environment...

THE "AWWWW" SCALE

Level 1:

Offense – Excessive meowing.
Pose – Nothing particular...just be yourself.
Human Response – "Awwww."

Level 2:

Offense – Overturned wastebasket.
Pose – Stare at human with big round eyes.
Human Response – "Awwwww."

Level 3:

Offense – Cat toys strewn around house.
Pose – Pounce on toys and bat them around.
Human Response – "Awwwwww."

Level 4:

Offense – Unraveled roll of toilet paper.
Pose – Lie in shredded paper with only head exposed.
Human Response – "Awwwwwww."

Level 5:

Offense – Shredding arm of couch.
Pose – Pause, flash mischievous look, bolt away.
Human Response – "Awwwwwwww."

Level 6:

Offense – Eating food from table.
Pose – Look up at human with food on muzzle.
Human Response – "Awwwwwwwww."

Level 7:

Offense – Destruction of houseplant.
Pose – Squint eyes, scrunch up face.
Human Response – "Awwwwwwwwww."

Level 8:

Offense – Destruction of valued item.
Pose – Lie on back, squint eyes, curl front paws.
Human Response – "Awwwwwwwwwww."

Level 9:

Offense – Scratching human.
Pose – Look contrite, meow softly and apologetically.
Human Response – "Awwwwwwwwwwww."

Level 10:

Offense – Starting World War III.
Pose – Cover face with paws and pray.
Human Response – "Awwwwwwwwwwwww."

Ways to Annoy Your Human Just for Fun

As all experienced cats know, there are times we must resort to what some might consider annoying methods to get what we want from our humans, be it food, attention, stock options... whatever. But sometimes, it's fun to engage in a bit of horseplay and bedevil your human purely for your own amusement. That's right... good old-fashioned taunting and teasing to get a rise out of your human and some good yuks for yourself. It's fun, it's easy, and it's way more entertaining than cleaning yourself.

Here are some classic ways to cheese off your human, merely for the fun of it...

Way Way in the Way: This is one of Piglet's favorites. Wait until your human is doing something that requires them to stand in one place for awhile, such as washing the dishes, then plop yourself down at their feet and refuse to move. This will require them to engage in some fancy footwork when reaching for the dish soap or putting silverware in the dishwasher or something like that, which to a human, is highly irritating. And if you get stepped on, be sure and let out a loud, heartrending screech (even if it didn't hurt) to make your human feel guilty for getting in YOUR way.

Make Me Wanna Holler: This is a good one for you cats with big voices and one of my personal favorites. Let's say your human is doing something that requires focus and concentration – reading, perhaps, or trying to repair something with minute parts – then park yourself in the middle of the floor and shout out a proclamation in your loudest, most stentorian voice. Wait ten seconds and do it again... and again and again and again and again. This will make concentration impossible for your human and totally disrupt whatever they were trying to do. What fun!

Shred 'N' Run: A classic. Go over to the couch (ignoring your scratching post on the way) and give the arm a good, noisy shred. Really work those claws so the rending and tearing can be heard throughout the house. When your human yells, "Stop it!" run away as if you are afraid they might actually do something to stop you. After they return to whatever it was they were doing, go back to the couch and pick up where you left off. When they yell at you again, quickly bolt away. Do this as many times as you want, or until you get bored. It's delightfully maddening to your human and allows you to get in a good scratch all at the same time.

What's On TV? Here's a good one if your human has an old school TV... in other words, one of those large old clunky sets with a big picture tube. Wait until your human is settled in watching a show, preferably one of their favorites, then jump up on top of the TV (as an added benefit, it will be nice and warm). Sit with your back to your human and let your tail fall lazily in front of the screen. Swish your tail slowly back and forth so that no matter where it is, it will block some portion of the action. Delightful! However, because most humans are switching to accursedly-thin flat screen TVs, which were clearly not designed with cats in mind, this enjoyable source of amusement will probably disappear over time and become part of feline lore... something grandma and grandpa kitties will nostalgically remember and tell kittens about.

Gimme Some Lap: Wait until your human is using their computer, then loudly announce that you want some lap time NOW. Before your human can react, jump up on their lap and get comfortable, making sure to occupy as much space as possible. If you're big enough, or if you spread yourself out enough, your human won't be able to reach the keyboard and continue working. After a couple token pets, they'll probably set you back down on the floor and get back to whatever they were doing. Simply jump up in their lap again... and again and again and again. This is one of B.D.'s personal favorites and rapidly becoming one of mine.

Hey, What's That You're Eating? Here's one that will probably earn you a good scolding, but well worth it in terms of the annoyance factor. Wait until your human is eating a big, delicious meal and really getting into it. Jump up on the table and proceed slowly toward the food for a look-see and a sniff. This will, no doubt, cause your human to scoop you up, plop you back down on the floor and give you a big lecture about how cats are not allowed on the table while humans are eating. When the tirade stops and your human returns to their food, jump up on the table again.... and again and again and... well, you know the drill. Highly vexing to your human and highly amusing for you. And if you're quick enough, you might even be able to grab something delicious before you're heaved off the table.

Maid Service Please! This one is so much fun and so highly irksome to humans, it's amazing more cats don't do it. When your human is making the bed and has pulled up the bottom sheet, jump up and plop yourself down. Because this will prevent them from smoothing out the sheet and continuing with the bed making process, they'll undoubtedly lift you down onto the floor. Wait 2.5 seconds, then jump up again and plop yourself down. By repeating this process over and over (and over and over and over), you will effectively stymie your human's effort to make the bed and cause extremely entertaining consternation.

Dematerialization: Another classic. Hide and make yourself impossible to find. Your human expects you to do this when something scary happens or if you're up for a visit to the vet... but if you hide for no apparent reason, you human will eventually wonder where you are and come looking for you. If you're extremely well hidden, your human will become extremely frustrated and waste loads of time trying to find you. As English and Canadian kitties would say... brilliant!

Cat Burglar: This one is so great, I get excited just thinking about it. Wait until your human inadvertently leaves a drawer open, like a dresser drawer, or even better, the drawer in a jewelry box. Slink up there like a creepy cat burglar, grab an object such as an earring, and bat it under the dresser or the bed. Then sit back and enjoy the turmoil as your human goes crazy trying to find the "missing" object.

Please, Sir, May I Have Some More? This is my all-time favorite. When your human is eating, sit on the floor and look up at them with your irresistible, pleading kitty eyes. That's right... the feline version of begging. It doesn't matter what your human is eating or whether you really want it. The object is to pester them to the point where they drop a little something on the floor for you to taste. Take a sniff or two, refuse to eat it, and give your human a "What the hay is this?" look. This will cause them to pick up whatever it was they gave you and throw it away. Wait until they resume eating, then "forget" that you didn't like what you were given and get back to begging. VERY entertaining!

So, fellow prankster, knock yourself out with these creative ways to drive your human to distraction just for the fun of it. Be sure to mix things up a bit... that way, you won't get bored and your human won't catch on to the fact that you're having a bit of sport with them.

Breezy Excuses for Unacceptable Kitty Behavior

I'm sure I don't need to tell you that all humans, even if they are proven cat nuts, will become quite angry if you push them too far and commit an act of unacceptable kitty behavior. What is considered unacceptable kitty behavior varies considerably from one human to another depending on their level of cat adulation. Still, pretty much all humans will draw a line in the sand at some point, and if you cross that line, you could find yourself – pardon the expression – in the doghouse.

In my first book, I provided an in-depth explanation on how to get away with unacceptable kitty behavior, and believe me fellow miscreant, this is definitely an area where you want to keep your chops up. You certainly don't want to let your how-to-get-away-with-unacceptable-kitty-behavior skills get rusty.

Still, there are instances when you might not have time to go through the hassle of looking cute or acting innocent just because of some minor infraction. You might have important work to do, like cleaning yourself or investigating the inside of a paper bag, or it might simply be time for a rejuvenating nap. Or like a spoiled child or a pre-rehab Hollywood actor, perhaps you just won't feel like taking responsibility for your actions.

For those occasions where time is of the essence, or when you just can't be bothered to provide a lengthy explanation for your transgression, here is a list of common kitty offenses and breezy one-line responses you can throw at your human before getting back to the task (or nap) at hand:

Offense	Breezy Excuse
"Accident"outside litter box.	The box was just TOO stinky.
Clawing arm of couch.	I needed a good scratch and my scratching post was all the way over in the next room.
Clawing screen door.	The spaces in the screen were too small to let in sufficient air.
Destruction of indoor houseplant.	It was giving off "bad vibes."
Destruction of outdoor plant.	It looked like a weed (to me, anyway).

Offense	Breezy Excuse
Destruction of valuable artifact.	It moved into my way while I was bolting around the house.
Destruction of female's shoes.	They were no longer in style.
Shredding of important document.	Homeland Security called and ordered me to do it.
Shredding of newspaper.	I was trying to keep you from becoming depressed by reading about the economy.
Shredding roll of toilet paper.	What else is toilet paper for?
Waking your human at 6:00 a.m.	I need some attention and food NOW.
Clawing carpet around closed door.	If I had opposable thumbs, I could have opened the door myself.
Walking on kitchen counters.	I'm on a really important reconnaissance mission.
Opening kitchen cabinets.	I'm looking for Osama bin Laden.

Offense	Breezy Excuse
Eating items in kitchen cabinets.	They looked more interesting and tasty than my normal food.
Lying on clean pile of laundry.	It's so nice and warm, I just couldn't resist.
Scratching and biting houseguests.	I hate them!
Knocking lamp over and breaking light bulb.	I'm trying to conserve energy.
Walking on computer keyboard.	I'm working on my memoirs.
Messing around on female's dressing table.	I'm looking for some nice earrings to wear.
Knocking over and rummaging through wastebasket.	I'm looking for good batting-around material.
Grabbing and biting human's arm during tummy rub.	I was momentarily possessed by Beelzebub.
Getting cat hair on human's clothing.	I want you to take a bit of me with you wherever you go (Awwwwww....).

Babysitting Guest Kittens

Awhile back, before the arrival of Bo Diddley and Piglet in our household, Steve's female decided (without asking Steve and me, of course) to take care of two very young kittens for a friend who was going away for the weekend. Now I'm a pretty agreeable and hospitable guy, but when I heard that two kittens would be staying at our house for a whole weekend, I was clearly not elated. Sure kittens are delightful, but two full days with a couple squalling, meddlesome hellions? I wouldn't have a moment's peace.

Still, there was one upside to all this, and that was watching the engaging, entertaining repartee between Steve and his female when she told him about the two kitten visitors. Naturally, she did it when Steve was weak and tired from a day's "work" and sprawled out on the couch nursing a beer. And as always, when the female makes a decision on her own, Steve attempts to put his foot down and assert his alpha maleness. It's sort of like watching the Chicago Cubs try and get into the World

Series—hard as they try, they always seem to fold in the end. Yet in the name of male bonding, I always root for Steve, futile as that may be. Here's how it went down between Steve and his female, with my comments in parenthesis:

> **Steve's Female**: We're going to be taking care of Ellen's kittens this weekend. (*Typical female tactic... just drop the bomb and catch the populace unawares.*)

> **Steve**: WHAT??? (*Extra entertainment as Steve sits up abruptly with beer shooting out of his nose.*)

> **Steve's Female**: Ellen's going away this weekend and I told her we'd take care of Smokey and Squirt. You don't mind, do you?

> **Steve**: Yes I mind! We can't take care of two kittens. (*Good comeback. En garde!*)

> **Steve's Female**: Why not? (*Uh-oh... the first parry.*)

> **Steve**: Because it'll be too much trouble. And besides, Quasi will hate it. (*Hey, bub, don't drag me into this.*)

> **Steve's Female**: Quasi won't mind. (*Oh yes I will.*) The kittens will play with him and he'll get some exercise for a change. (*WHAT!*) And why will it be too much trouble?

> **Steve**: Because... oh, I don't know. It'll just be too much of a hassle. (*Oh, great response. We might as well beat our swords into ploughshares right now.*)

Steve's Female: I really don't see what the big problem is. And they're SOOOOO cute.

Steve: Well... (*Quick. Call the seismological reinforcement company. The foundation is weakening.*)

Steve's Female: Think how much fun we'll have watching Quasi and the kittens interact. (*Fun for you, maybe.*)

Steve: Well... I guess...

Steve's Female: Oh, thank you! I knew you'd see it my way.

And so, on Friday night, just after dinner, Smokey and Squirt, the two guest kittens, came over. Smokey is all gray (hence his name), and Squirt is tiger-stripped and very small (hence his name).

Now, first let me say this: yes, kittens ARE very cute—from a human's perspective, that is. Humans love their adorable little faces, their tiny peeping voices, their unbridled curiosity and boundless kitten energy, their bumbling attempts at agility, their youthful naïveté. Admittedly, it's not hard to see how a gushy cat-loving human can be instantly overcome and reduced to a puddle of goo by a kitten's cuteness.

But let's look at it from the perspective of an adult cat—in other words, from MY perspective. Cuteness aside, kittens are a big pain in the hindquarters. First of all, they're bothersome little rapscallions. No matter what you're doing, they always want to "help." They think all objects, living or otherwise, were put on earth purely for their own amusement. They're not happy unless they're creating some kind of hubbub. And all they want to do is PLAY, PLAY, PLAY.

As expected, the mayhem ensued from the moment Smokey and Squirt bolted out of their cat carrier. First they cased the joint, poking their snoopy little kitten noses into everything, including my personal stuff. My favorite paper bag, which I worked so hard to get just right, was completely thrashed and mutilated. All my toy mice were recklessly batted under the refrigerator. My carefully chosen sleeping spots and hiding places were wantonly desecrated. Every other minute, I was pummeled in a kitty stampede as these two little devils chased each other from one end of the house to the other, flying over or crashing into everything in their way. Their mewling little voices made sleep impossible, resulting in sleep deprivation that made me even grouchier than I already was.

And naturally, I couldn't even twitch without drawing kitten fire. If I moved my tail just one fraction of a millimeter, one of them would pounce on it and sometimes even bite it with their sharp little kitten teeth. Talk about annoying. Don't they realize I have important adult cat work to do? Who do they think does all the investigative work around here? The cast from CSI? Who do they think supervises Steve and his female and prevents them from making cataclysmic mistakes that could affect the entire household? Who do they think keeps the yard free of bugs, birds and enemy cats?

But worst of all, these interlopers deflected attention away from ME. Yes, even my time-tested kitty cuteness was no match for these little bundles of fluff, especially with Steve's female, who fawned and cooed over them like a teenage girl at a Justin Bieber concert. And if all this wasn't bad enough, when Smokey and Squirt used the litter box—*Madre de Dios.* It's hard to believe such tiny, delicate creatures could create such an unearthly stench!

Regardless of my concerns, I was stuck with Smokey and Squirt until Sunday evening. All my normal efforts to restore order failed miserably. Hissing did nothing to deter these frisky little imps, and whapping them on the head only caused the female to become more protective of them and look on me as a callous, kitten-abusing brute. As you can imagine, fellow adult cat, serious action was needed to right the ship.

Because I was much smarter and craftier than Smokey and Squirt in their callow youth, I came up with a plan that was so inspired yet simple, I couldn't believe I didn't think of it right away. All I had to do was use the kittens' own shenanigans – with a little help from me, of course – to get them in deep trouble and make Steve and the female realize, especially the female, that babysitting these two little monsters was a horrible mistake. In other words, just teach the kittens how to use their destructive potential to its fullest, then sit back and watch the repercussions.

I waited for Steve and his female to leave the house— then I went to work.

The first thing I did was to teach Smokey and Squirt how to unravel an entire roll of toilet paper. They were immediately captivated by the delightful rumbling sound the roller made as the paper tumbled onto the floor in a glorious pile. Then I encouraged them to shred the toilet paper into pieces no larger than one inch square, and to strew the confetti all around the bathroom. What fun!

Next, I taught the kittens the joys of chewing on the leaves of houseplants and digging in the dirt, making sure to fling most of it onto the carpet. And speaking of digging in the dirt, I told them that there was really no need to go all the way to the litter box when they had to do their little kitty business, the dirt made a handy and much more convenient substitute.

Then I taught Smokey and Squirt some advanced techniques for sharpening their claws on the arm of the couch, including the all-important back flex and my patented two-pawed march-and-rip approach. I explained that scratching posts were for sissies, and that real cats ALWAYS used the arm of the couch.

Smokey and Squirt were so excited to learn all this, they looked up at me with their eager little kitty faces as if to say, "Oh, thank you, Quasi. Please teach us some more!"

No problemo, gatitos pequeños. How about going into the kitchen cupboards (opened surreptitiously by me) and tearing into a few packages of pasta, flour, and other food stuffs? How about chewing on a pair of the female's new shoes (and leaving conspicuous, telltale kitten teeth marks all over them)? How about selectively shredding the sports page of the newspaper (leaving the boring sections untouched, as suggested by yours truly), making it impossible for Steve to read about the latest steroids scandal involving overpaid athletes? How about jumping up on the bookshelf and pushing all the books out onto the floor (need help with the heavy ones? Just call on 'ole Quaz). How about knocking over a lamp or two? How about climbing up the curtains and making a multitude of little holes with your claws? How about upending every wastebasket in the house and playing "kitty soccer" with the detritus?

Yes, Smokey and Squirt took to their "lessons" with youthful alacrity and surprising skill. In a matter of just a few hours, they came close to reaching their full destructive potential, although they still had a long way to go before they would reach the penultimate kitty destruction level I attained during my legendary kittenhood. And in the spirit of brotherhood, as the sun set over the smoldering ruins, I invited Smokey and Squirt to take a much needed nap with me (and wait for Steve and his female to come home—heh, heh!)

Here's how it went when Steve and the female walked through the door and saw the carnage, (again with my comments in parentheses)...

Steve: What the...????

Steve's Female: Oh. My. Gawd. It looks like a tornado went through here. (*Ah, yes... the desired response.*)

Steve: Uh-oh... you better come look at this.

Steve's Female: Oh, no! They've pooped in the plants (*I told them to use the litter box, but they just wouldn't listen.*) And they've gotten into everything in the kitchen. There's flour and pasta everywhere. (*Gadzooks... what would Emeril say?*) And look at the bathroom. They've shredded an entire roll of toilet paper. (*Walkin' in a win-ter wonderland.*)

Steve: Well, I told you it would be a big hassle having two kittens around. (*That's right. Let the* *female know she should have listened to you. Surely it will make a HUGE DIFFERENCE the next time she wants to do something and you don't.*)

Steve's Female: I just don't understand it. They were so sweet and good this morning when we were around. What could've happened? (*Beats the heck out of me.*)

Steve: I told you....

Of course, Smokey and Squirt didn't get into any real trouble despite the near-historic level of devastation and ruin... their overwhelming kitten cuteness prevented them from incurring any serious repercussions. The female realized that babysitting two kittens wasn't such a great idea after all, and Steve had the smug satisfaction of knowing that he was right (for the moment anyway). Needless to say, no one suspected that I had ANYTHING to do with the mini-disaster. And in the end, I saved Smokey and Squirt a lot of time by teaching them so many kitten antics in one sitting. Otherwise, it would have taken them weeks to figure all this stuff out.

So, fellow full-grown cat, if you ever find yourself in a similar situation where a couple kittens are foisted off on you, just teach them the fine art of havoc and let the chips fall where they may. Sure, there may be a certain amount of collateral damage, but sometimes drastic measures must be taken to teach your human a lesson they shan't soon forget.

More Humans' Questions about Cats

In my first book, in an attempt to answer ages-old human questions about cats and clue them in on what makes us kitties tick, I included a chapter entitled "Humans' Questions about Cats." While this helped to clear up some of the mysteries of kittydom for our humans' sake, I subsequently realized that many unanswered questions remained. So, in an effort to further advance human knowledge of *felinus domesticus,* (that's 'cats' for you kitties who didn't take Latin in school), here are even more humans' questions about cats and the irrefutable answers....

Q. Do cats always land on their feet?
A. Yes (Well, most of the time).

Q. Do cats use their whiskers as feelers?
A. Yes.

Q. Do cats need catnip to relieve pressure and keep them sane?
A. Yes (Definitely!).

Q. Do cats lick themselves because they taste good?

A. Yes.

Q. Will cats turn into ungainly rubes if they eat dog food?

A. Yes.

Q. Will putting garlic on a cat's food keep vampires away?

A. Yes.

Q. Do cats go psycho at times merely to keep their humans on their toes?

A. Yes.

Q. Are cats required by law to wake their humans at a particular time?

A. Yes.

Q. Do cats prefer the arm of the couch to a scratching post?

A. Yes (Duh!).

Q. Should cats be given at least 12 cans of cat food a day?

A. Yes.

Q. Do cats see in hi-def?

A. Yes.

Q. Do cats know that within 30 years, the polar icecaps will melt and create beachfront property in Wichita, Kansas?

A. Yes.

Q. Do cats like to "freestyle" to crunk music?

A. Yes.

Q. Do all cats know the meaning of every word in the Oxford English Dictionary?

A. Yes.

Q. Do cats like to swim and splash around in water?

A. No (This is a joke, right?).

Q. Do cats like it when their breath smells like clam dip?

A. Yes.

Q. Do cats like movies with complicated romantic twists?

A. Yes.

Q. Do cats think that anyone who mistreats animals, dogs included, should be fricasseed?

A. Yes.

Q. Do cats use mind control on their humans?

A. Yes.

Q. Do cats stare at their humans merely to freak them out?

A. Yes.

Q. Do cats get on the computer at night and rearrange their human's Netflix queue?

A. Yes.

Q. Do cats know what really killed off the dinosaurs?

A. Yes.

Q. Do cats enter the fifth dimension to hide from their humans?

A. Yes.

Q. Do all cats, even little pipsqueaks like Piglet, think they are THE king of the jungle?

A. Yes.

Q. Do cats have the potential to become demented evil scientists like in old horror movies?

A. Yes.

Q. Do cats hear ultra-high frequencies in emo music that make their brains bubble?

A. Yes.

Q. Do cats dig in their litter boxes in hopes of finding buried treasure?

A. Yes.

Q. Do cats enjoy a good gladiator fight?

A. Yes.

Q. Are cats the best animals on earth?

A. Yes.

Q. Although they may not act like it at times, do cats actually think their humans are pretty special?

A. Possibly (Just kidding... of course we do!).

Things to Do (And Not Do) When You're Buzzed on Catnip

WARNING

The following chapter contains catnip-related material that may be unsuitable for kittens and cats under the age of 18 (in cat years).

READ AT YOUR OWN RISK!!!!

Sometimes, when the rigors of my complex life become too much to bear, I like to engage in a bit of escapism and lose myself in the glorious dreamlike high of catnip. Ahhh, the mind-altering, consciousness-elevating journey into the idyllic unknown, the summer-of-love groovy vibes, the psychedelic music (which has been pre-programmed into the iPod section of my kitty brain), the whirlwind of colors, the dancing, blissed out hippie chicks. One pill makes you larger and one pill makes you small indeed.

Now before you go getting the wrong idea, I would like to state, clearly and unequivocally, that I am NOT a wanton catnip abuser. I never use catnip first thing in the morning. I don't hide stashes of catnip around the house for a quick "nip" when no one is looking. I don't let catnip interfere with my kitty responsibilities around the homestead. I don't blame catnip for my problems or maladjustments (not that I have any). In other words, I'm not a waste-oid, a niphead or a layabout. I partake of catnip responsibly and only when the time is right.

Most human cat lovers keep a good supply of catnip around because they think it's amusing to watch us kitties get high and act like whacked-out flower children from the hippie days. And you know what? It is amusing, for them AND for us. Catnip brings cats and humans together. We get a nice buzz and they get a few cheap laughs. It's a win-win situation for everyone. What could be better?

Recently, Steve came home with a great new catnip toy. Although it's officially called "Deluxe Hot Cat," I call it "The Sausage." The toy is basically four material-covered cylinders linked together in a manner similar to sausages (hence the nickname). However, instead of being filled with repulsive, unspeakable God-knows-what like real sausage cylinders, my new toy is filled with – yes, that's right – CATNIP. Oh, the joy of rolling, sniffing and licking my way from one cylinder to the next. Plus, because of its length, I can rub one end of "The Sausage" around my face while gripping and kicking at the other end with my hind legs. This has got to be the best human invention yet. The wheel, the electric light bulb, TV and penicillin pale in comparison. (Okay, Mr. Manufacturer of Deluxe Hot Cat, I'm ready to consider your endorsement offer now.)

Why does catnip have such an effect on us? Well, according to Wikipedia, catnip comes from the plant genus Nepeta. This genus contains an organic compound known as nepatalactone, which is detected by a specialized epithelial tissue inside a cat's nasal cavity and sends us into a frenzy of ecstasy... or something like that. But who cares about all this scientific and horticultural mumbo-jumbo? The point, fellow cat, is to make certain that your human NEVER runs out of catnip. After all, when you feel a need to escape from pesky reality, you don't want to have to resort to Yoga or transcendental meditation or some other boring substitute for just plain getting blasted. And be sure you have plenty of food in your bowl (or in an accessible cupboard) for when the munchies strike.

Here are some fun things to do when you're buzzed on catnip:

- ❖ Chase imaginary birds and bugs.

- ❖ Stare at an orange for five-and-a-half hours.

- ❖ Listen for secret messages from the underworld on your human's death metal CDs.

- ❖ Sit on the back of the couch with your eyes half closed and a Cheshire Cat grin on your face.

- ❖ Stand on your hind legs and play air guitar.

- ❖ Think deep thoughts that seem meaningful to your catnip-addled brain, but are, in reality, nothing but ridiculous nonsense.

- ❖ Bolt erratically around the house.

- ❖ Dance the Hokey-Pokey.

- ❖ Listen to every Bob Marley song ever recorded.

- ❖ Dream up wonderful ways you could wreak havoc if you had opposable thumbs.

- ❖ Laugh uncontrollably at things that are not really funny.

- ❖ Watch the news on TV and pretend all the commentators have cat heads.

- ❖ Speak in tongues.

- ❖ Float 38,000 feet above your city or town (in your mind, that is).

- ❖ Engage in telepathic communication with other stoned cats on the planet Xandor.

And as a public service announcement and word of warning, here are some things you should NOT do when you're under the influence of catnip:

- ❖ Play in the street.

- ❖ Climb up a tree with an eagle's nest at the top.

- ❖ Explore the inside of a thermonuclear reactor.

- ❖ Go up to a cop and say, "Pardon me officer, but do I look high to you?"

- ❖ Eat anything from a container marked with a scary human skull.

- ❖ Challenge a large dog (or a bigger cat) to pawsticuffs.

- ❖ Stick a claw into an electrical outlet.

- ❖ Stare directly into the Sun.

❖ Get stuck inside your chimney while looking for Santa Claus.

❖ Fall asleep in your litter box.

So there you have it, fellow nipster...several inspired ideas for making your next catnip blitz-a-thon even more pleasurable. Just remember to stay out of trouble and not try anything too tricky or complicated when you're abuzz. And like your 'ole pal Quasi... always make sure to use catnip sensibly and judiciously.

What to Do If Your Human Puts You on a Diet

For years, female humans have obsessed about their weight, often asking their male humans rhetorical questions like, "Do I look fat to you?" As if some male human would be stupid enough to say, "Yeah, you could stand to lose a few pounds." Even if a female human was as big as all outdoors, any male human that responded to a "fat" question with anything other than an emphatic "No!" would be asking for trouble on a nuclear scale.

When Steve's female concludes that she needs to shed some poundage, she goes on something called a "diet." From what I can determine, a diet involves giving up good food like hamburgers and pizza and replacing it with boring food such as salad and tofu (yucko) until the desired weight loss is achieved. Of course, this makes Steve's female inordinately cranky, which in turn makes Steve's life (and mine) miserable. And if Steve tries to eat any good food around the female, she glares at him with a look that says, "How DARE you enjoy yourself while I suffer to make myself more attractive for you."

No, fellow cat, it's not a pretty picture. But it can get much, much worse. Oh, yes. Just imagine that the diet victim is... YOU.

For some reason, many humans think we cats should be svelte, trim and toned up like a gym rat that spends 17 hours a day lifting weights and preening in front of a mirror. Some cats, like me, for instance, are big boned and prone to a little expanse, so how can we help it if we put on an extra pound or two... or three or four? Where do humans think the expression "Fat Cat" came from? Besides, who wants to look like a skeletal fashion model anyway?

Let me tell you a little story about what happened when Steve and the female tried to put ME on a diet... and how I rose to the occasion and thwarted their every effort.

A couple years back, when I was still the lone kitty in the household, Steve took me to the hated vet for my annual physical and shots (ouch!). As usual, it was wicked scary. The humiliating shove into the kitty carrier, the death-defying drive to the painmaster's office on the mean streets of Burbank, the endless wait to see the "doctor" while surrounded by other terrorized cats and yowling, slathering dogs.

But the worst part of the visit was at the very end of my examination/torture session, when the painmaster told Steve, "Quasi is in very good health except for one thing... he's obese. He could stand to lose three or four pounds."

Obese? No way!

"Quasi needs to be on 'lite' cat food for awhile. And you'll have to cut his dry food by about two thirds."

You CAN'T be serious. I'll waste away to nothing.

"And he could use more exercise."

More exercise? How will I sleep 20 hours a day and work on my plan for world peace if I have to waste time chasing a fake mouse or some wiggly cat toy?

But, alas. On the way out of the vet's office, Steve picked up a case of expensive "lite" specially-formulated diet cat food with the name "Duck & Green Peas." Gag-O-Rama! Clearly, I wasn't going to eat any of THAT.

Right about here, you're probably thinking, "Geez, Quaz, this diet thing sounds mighty unpleasant. What if my human does this to me?"

Well, if you're a plus-size cat like me, have no fear. As usual, I came up with an inventive solution to circumvent this ill-conceived diet concept and keep my stomach full of delicious, fattening food despite the best efforts of Steve and his female to turn me into one of the Olson twins.

Obviously, the first thing I did when Steve spooned some "Duck & Green Peas" into my bowl was to turn up my nose and refuse to eat any of it.

Steve expected this reaction, so he was not surprised. "Okay, Quaz, don't eat it, but don't think I'm gonna cave in and give you something else. You heard what the vet said. You're fat and you need to lose weight."

"Hurrumph," I grumbled, pirouetting away from my food bowl like Baryshnikov. I went to the front door and demanded to be let out. Steve came over and complied. However, he couldn't resist one snarky little, "Don't pass out from hunger out there, ha- ha."

"Real funny, Steve," I thought... but I already had a plan.

Under normal circumstances, I would have relied on the "In-and-Out" method of getting different food, as described in my first book. That is, you go to your food bowl, sniff the food disdainfully and turn up your nose, march to the door and demand to be let outside. Once your human lets you out, wait about 30 seconds, then demand to be let back in. Return to your food bowl, sniff the contents disdainfully and turn up your nose, march to the front door and demand to be let outside. Repeat the process again and again... and again and again. Very few humans can withstand this time-tested, scientifically-proven technique without cracking like an egg and giving you something good to eat.

This time, however, the stakes were much higher. I was on a diet and Steve had paid *mucho dinero* for my lite specially-formulated cat food. Plus, the female, a professional dieter, was in on it. Clearly the situation called for bigger, bolder action.

I set out for a little turn around the neighborhood, and using my method acting skills, acquired from watching Daniel Day-Lewis movies, I assumed the role of a wretched, hungry waif in Dickensian England, walking the dirty cobblestone streets in search of food. I headed straight to the home of Mrs. Anderson, who lived a couple doors down and knew me well. Mrs. Anderson was a kindly, elderly woman and a major cat lover, and because she had kitties of her own, I knew she would have normal, high-caloric (and delicious) cat food. I plopped down on her doorstep, and looking as pitiful as possible, wailed like a little lost orphan. Sure enough, Mrs. Anderson came to the door and smiled when she saw me.

"Why, hello there, Quasi," she said, bending down to give me a nice pat on the head. "What are you doing over here?"

I looked up at Mrs. Anderson with my limpid kitty eyes and meowed plaintively as if to say, "My cruel humans won't give me anything to eat and I'm SOOOO hungry." Being the perceptive cat nut that she is, she quickly got the gist of what I was saying.

"I guess Fluff and Misty can spare a little food for you, Quasi. Wait right there."

Oh, yes, come to papa!

Sure enough, Mrs. Anderson returned with a heaping bowl of Ocean Whitefish Treat, one of my personal favorites. I was on it before the bowl touched the ground.

"My," said Mrs. Anderson. "You certainly ARE hungry. Doesn't Steve feed you enough?"

Not hardly, I thought. I licked the bowl clean, and to make sure Mrs. Anderson would be receptive to future visits, I wove sinuously around her legs a few times and let her pick me up and cuddle me like a baby. Then I left and took a nice three hour nap under a bush so that by the time I went home, Steve wouldn't smell the Ocean Whitefish Treat on my breath.

Thanks to Mrs. Anderson's largess over the next few weeks, I was able to eat like a food critic while on my diet. To ensure that Steve and his female wouldn't get suspicious at meal times, I always made sure to spread my lite kitty food around the bowl so it looked like I had actually eaten some of it. I also backed off my usual quantity of food just a bit so I would actually lose a quarter pound here and there. This is difficult, but very important because if you don't lose at least a little weight, even the dumbest human will eventually figure out that you're getting food somewhere else.

Ultimately, as I knew it would, the hassle of keeping me on a diet became too much for Steve and his female.

Because I had actually lost a half a pound or so over the course of my diet, they decided that was pretty much good enough and accepted the fact that I'm just a big guy. Plus, I'm sure Steve was only too glad to stop shelling out *beaucoup* bucks for my "Duck & Green Peas" diet food.

Cats 1, Humans 0.

Now at this juncture, you're probably thinking, "Hey, Quasi, that's real nice, but what if I get put on a diet and I don't have a kindly human in the neighborhood that I can con into giving me palatable food?"

No problem, fellow gourmand. Because many humans are too lazy to get up and expend the 1.5 calories necessary to walk to the door and let their cats outside, some have installed pet doors so their kitties can come and go at will. Simply wander around your 'hood until you find a home with a pet door, then head on in and scarf down whatever you can find. A word of warning here, though... before you undertake any cat burglar-type action like this, make sure the cat of the house is away (or napping soundly). You certainly don't want some macho, rough-tough tomcat to stroll in and find you with your face buried in his food bowl. That would NOT be a good thing. If this does happen, quickly act you're sleepwalking and don't know where you are or how you got there. Or start jabbering in tongues like you're dangerously crazy. Or pretend you're a food inspector, and with an authoritarian air (as you're backing toward the exit) say something to the effect of, "I'm from the Health Department. This food is spoiled. I'm afraid I'm going to have to report you." Situations like this call for quick thinking, so to avoid a good butt-kicking, make sure to have a creative response at the ready.

If you're an indoor cat and your human puts you on a diet, you've got a slightly more difficult task ahead of you, but not to worry. You've got a full arsenal of exasperating kitty tricks at your disposal, and if you use them appropriately, you should have no trouble convincing your human that putting you on a diet is a very bad idea. Here's what to do...

When your human dumps some inedible diet-type food in your bowl, turn up your nose and refuse to eat any of it. Give your human a "thanks for nothing" look, and then march away in disgust. However, instead of going to the door and yowling to be let outside, follow your human around the house wherever they may go, all the while meowing and looking as pathetic and hungry as possible. Use every word in your vocabulary and pump some volume into it. Every so often, stroll into the kitchen, or wherever your food bowl is located, and caterwaul mournfully to make sure your human understands why you're upset, and that you mean business. If they try to watch TV or read or do anything else that requires concentration, make concentration impossible. Pace around the room, claw the arm of the couch, knock over a few tchotchkes... whatever. If they toss you in another room and close the door, hurl yourself the door repeatedly and howl like a werewolf. The point is, fellow cat, you want to let your human know, without question, that there will be – yes, that's right – NO PEACE ON EARTH until they drop this ill-advised diet idea and give you some decent food to eat. Bear in mind that you may have to keep this up for two or three days... some humans can be pretty stubborn when it comes to diets. But eventually, I can assure you, even the most steadfast human will snap like a dry twig and bow to your will.

So as you can see, fellow *gatos grandes*, there are several sure-fire ways to outwit your human if they try to force you to lose weight. Remember, diets are for supermodels, athletes, and human males and females who are willing to torture themselves to look appealing to members of the opposite sex. But you know what? If God wanted cats to be skinny, he (or she) wouldn't have made cat food so sumptuously delicious.

> **NOTE 1:** No matter how hungry you may become, do not eat garbage. While there's a chance you might find something decent, you also might chow down on something that will make you sick, necessitating a trip to the dreaded vet (gulp).

> **NOTE 2:** If you decide on your own that you want to tone up and lose weight, that's a different situation because YOU made the decision as opposed to being the victim of a conspiracy between your human and the vet. But if you're a little on the large side and want to remain the roly-poly ball of confusion that you are, don't let ANY mortal deprive you of your right to be rotund, your choice to be chunky, your prerogative to be plump, or your freedom to be just plain old fat.

20 Reasons Why Cats Are Smarter Than Humans

Want to know what really gets my pet dander up? What really chafes my hind end? What really makes me want to scream and shout and knock myself out? It's when I do something so simple a monkey (or a dog) could do it, and then Steve says in stunned amazement, "Wow, Quasi is really smart!"

What does he take me for? A blockhead? A mental midget? An ignoramus? Of course I'm really smart. My kitty brain is filled to capacity and bubbling over with knowledge that would make a college professor pale in comparison. Just because I don't flaunt it doesn't mean I'm not a genius (if I don't say so myself).

What many humans fail to realize is that ALL cats are smart. In fact, we're so smart, we disguise our intelligence so we can spend the majority of the day napping and playing. If our humans knew how smart we really are, they'd shirk their responsibilities and we'd have to do everything.

Still, no self-respecting cat likes being treated like a dunce, so for your human's edification, here are 20 good reasons why cats are smarter than humans...

1. Cats don't smoke cigarettes or drink alcohol.

2. Cats don't use recreational drugs (except catnip).

3. Cats don't drink gallons of coffee every morning and get hopped up on caffeine.

4. Cats don't cheat at cards and get into gun fights.

5. Cats don't go to crowded shopping malls at Christmas (or at any other time for that matter).

6. Cats don't rip off their fellow felines with shady financial schemes.

7. Cats don't run up exorbitant credit card bills.

8. Cats don't contribute to global warming (except when gas escapes from that tiny hole at the base of our tails).

9. Cats don't have complicated interpersonal relationships that require constant maintenance.

10. Cats don't commit crimes and wind up in jail.

11. Cats don't start wars (except with other cats).

12. Cats don't invent annoying products like leaf blowers.

13. Cats don't do ridiculously-dangerous things like mountain climbing or skydiving (although, admittedly, we do get ourselves into some pretty harrowing situations from time to time).

14. Cats don't take performance-enhancing drugs in order to hit more home runs.

15. Cats don't text while hurtling down the highway at mind-numbing speeds.

16. Cats don't engage in risky scientific endeavors like splitting the atom or blowing holes in the ozone layer.

17. Cats don't have unnecessary plastic surgery that makes them look like cartoon characters.

18. Cats don't worry or care about what is socially acceptable and what is not.

19. Cats don't squander natural resources (except maybe cat food when we don't like what's been served).

20. Cats don't need to go to college because they already know everything.

How to Make Sure Your Human Keeps Your Litter Box Clean

It goes without saying that one thing we cats simply cannot abide is a litter box that is not up to our rigorous standards of hygiene and cleanliness. There's nothing more disgusting than walking into a litter box that – well, there's just no nice way to say it – is a sickening, revolting mess. No cat wants to use a litter box that looks like a Superfund site or an annex to the city dump. And let's face it... sometimes our humans are a little less than diligent when it comes to keeping our litter boxes tidy. So like most matters involving your human, you must take command of the situation and make sure your human keeps your litter box at least as clean as the men's room at a Shell station (which, in some cases, is not asking a lot).

The first and most obvious way to let your human know that your litter box needs cleaning is to have an "accident" outside the box. This will undoubtedly cause your human to become very upset and question why you had such an egregious lapse in your *toilette* routine. When they start berating you about your indiscretion, give them a pathetic look and a heartrending little meow that says, "I'm SOOO sorry, but my litter box was too dirty and unsanitary for me to use and I just couldn't hold it any longer." At this point, most humans will immediately feel guilty about their lapse in keeping your litter box clean and they'll rectify the situation posthaste. Of course, in instances like this, you want to make sure your box is really dirty, and that your "accident" was justified. Otherwise, you'll merely get a good scolding and the condition in your litter box will not improve. Still, this is usually enough to get the point across and prompt most semi-diligent humans to get busy on the cleanup operation. Yes, fellow sanitary engineer, there are times where you have to THINK outside the litter box, and there are times where you have to ACT outside the litter box.

Unfortunately, though, there are some humans who are just naturally slobs and won't connect the dots between your "accident" and the need to clean your litter box. If your human falls into this category, you must take the battle to the next level and either increase the number of "accidents" outside the box or take your "accidents" on the road – that is, to other parts of the house, and preferably on or near one of your human's prized possessions. This will cause even the most dimwitted (and messiest) human to consider the possibility that maybe – just maybe – your litter box needs a thorough cleaning.

Here's another good (and fun) way to make sure your human keeps your litter box fresh and clean. Simply get in there and start a major excavation project. For added excitement, pretend you're Indiana Jones on an archeological dig unearthing priceless relics. Hey, who knows... you might actually find something interesting. Or, if you like, you can pretend you're a construction worker digging the foundation for a dynamic new high rise building. Dig down with gusto and don't be shy about flinging lots of litter out of the box. In fact, if you fling just about all the litter out, your human will have no choice but to replace it with new, untainted litter.

If all else fails, try this... when leaving a deposit in the bank of litter box, make sure to leave one that is extra large and stinky. And don't bother to cover it up. When you're done, stand outside the litter box for a few minutes and swish your tail back and forth. This will cause the "aroma" to waft out into the rest of the house and make things mighty unpleasant for the other occupants. Unless your human was a disco freak or a heavy metal rocker back in the day and burned out their nasal passages by snorting all sorts of chemical inebriants, their sense of smell will tell them that significant clean up work is required and cannot wait another minute.

Yes, fellow cat, litter box issues can be a messy problem for sure, but I guarantee you that one, if not all three of these viable solutions, will inspire your human to keep your litter box as spotless and sanitary as an operating room (well, maybe not THAT clean).

NOTE 1: Don't let your human cheap out and buy inferior grade cat litter to save a few bucks. If they dump some litter into your box that fails to meet your USDA kitty standards of approval, don't use it. You heard right. Do your business outside the box or in a houseplant if you have to. You must make your human understand that no corners are to be cut when it comes to your litter box.

NOTE 2: Some humans will let your litter go a few days longer by trying to mask the odor with scented candles or air fresheners. Nice try, bucko! All cats know that there is nothing – NOTHING – that can cover the smell of a dirty litter box.

NOTE 3: Don't let your human make snide, untoward comments about the fragrance of your deposits in the litter box. If they do, let them know that their business wouldn't smell so good either if all they ate was offal (delicious as it may be).

How to Deal with Precocious Little Humans (Yes, That's Right – Children)

Of the many things a cat must deal with during the course of daily life, there are few things more vexing than children humans. Why, you ask? Well, to begin with, children take attention away from cats, and that in and of itself is bad enough. Some delusional humans even think babies are cuter than cats... can you believe it? Also, babies cry, screech, and make other unearthly sounds at a volume level equivalent to a White Stripes concert. It's hard to believe that creatures with such tiny lungs can create such a din. How can any cat sleep through that?

And then there are all those ridiculous old wives tales about cats and newborn babies. One is that cats dislike the smell of an infant's breath and therefore will try to harm them. That's disingenuous tommy rot. Personally, I love the smell of strained squash and asparagus on a baby's breath. Then there's the classic about a cat sucking out an infant's breath while the baby is sleeping. Talk about fear mongering. Who comes up with this stuff anyway?

I've even heard of families that believe this nonsense and get rid of their cat when a newborn arrives for fear that the cat would do something horrible to their precious little future doctor or whatever.

Let me, right here and now, put those ugly rumors to bed. We cats would never do anything to harm an infant. What kind of ogres do humans think we are? Oh sure, we'll definitely check out babies while they're sleeping (probably the source of the rumor that we're trying to steal their breath) and maybe even administer a few harmless exploratory whaps just to see what happens... but we cats have nothing but good intentions (and curiosity) toward new-to-the-world humans.

Now, having said that, let me return to the problem at hand, and that is, the problems children cause for cats and how to deal with the situation.

First, as I mentioned a moment ago, most humans turn all mushy and gooey in the presence of a newborn baby. It's very similar to what happens when a human succumbs to our kitty cuteness, only it's much worse with an infant because a baby is basically a miniature version of a full-grown human, and let's face it... most creatures prefer their own species to others. Quite frankly, I don't understand all the fuss. To me, all human babies look like bulbous blobs of Silly Putty and they're not anywhere near as cute as a kitten. Infants wake up in the middle of the night and make a devilish racket until someone gets up and tends to them. They constantly drool and spit up, which is messy and disgusting, and when they eat, they get food all over their faces. Don't they understand that the object is to get the food into their mouth? And babies don't even have any fur to keep them warm!

Regardless, if a newborn human comes into your house, your human will undoubtedly make a big fuss over them, and in some cases, they may ignore you and shunt you aside like so much chattel.

Don't let this happen to you.

If your human is gushing over a baby and disregarding you, you must first let them know that baby or not, you are *numero uno* and will not be ignored. Start by sitting in the middle of the room and speaking in a sweet, yet firm voice. If they continue to ignore you, speak louder and more forcefully. Use whatever cute inflections you have in your vocal repertoire and keep it up. Breathy meows, chirps, comical howls... whatever. The message you want to convey is, quite simply, "Pay attention to MEEEEE." If your human is a true cat nut, this will usually work, or at least get you noticed and maybe patted on the head. But we're not looking for perfunctory gestures of affection here. Oh, no. When we cats want some good lovin,' we want – dare I say it? – the lion's share.

If the mere sound of your voice does not get your human to do your bidding, saunter over to them and, while still speaking, wind yourself sinuously around their legs. Again, if your human is a major cat lover, they'll probably reach down and give you a nice little pat to let you know they still care about you. However, if they're holding the infant at the time, they may think you're trying to trip them and make them drop the baby, which will probably make them angry and cause them to yell at you, so be careful.

If none of this works, jump up into the infant's cradle and settle in for a nice nap. If a soft, warm baby blanket is available, shove your face into it for a good, soothing nuzzle. If the infant is not there, your human will probably consider this an "awwww" moment and realize that they've been paying attention too much attention to the wrong mammal. If the baby is in the crib at the time, though, they'll probably go berserk, grab you and toss you out for fear that you'll do something sinister to the little tot.

If this happens, walk a few paces away, assume your favorite cute cat pose, and pout as only a cat can. If your human comes over to beg your forgiveness, show them your hind end and walk away. If they follow you and pick you up for an "I'm sorry" cuddle, squirm out of their grasp and maybe even give them a little hiss for good measure. The point you want to make, emphatically if necessary, is... it's the baby or me. Now, between us cats, the fact is that you'll probably have to compromise a bit here (I know... compromise? What's that?), because chances are, they're not going to get rid of the baby. Still, you don't want your human to think you'll play second fiddle to an infant or anything else, so when they pay more attention to the baby than you, you must assert your rights as the pet in the house.

Now, what about older children? This is where things can get really tricky, because from a cat's perspective, some – not all, mind you – but some children can be very precocious, and in some cases, even a little dangerous.

Webster's Dictionary defines "precocious" as a child who exhibits mature behavior at a very early age. That's merely a polite way of saying a child is spoiled, snotty and self-absorbed... in other words, more human-like at an early age.

Some parents think their child can do no wrong and encourage this type of behavior, which makes life miserable for cats (and all other living creatures) who come in contact with the child. Let me give you an example.

Steve and the female have a friend who is a single mom with a five-year-old boy named Micah. Micah's mother gushes over everything he does and never gets angry at him, no matter what kind of mayhem he might unleash. As far as she's concerned, the world revolves around Micah (which I know to be untrue because the world revolves around ME and there can be only one axis). If Micah scribbles on a piece of paper with a crayon, his mother thinks he's the next Picasso. If he flails away at Steve's guitar, she thinks he's the next Eric Clapton. If he makes an observation about something, she thinks he's the next deep thinker like Einstein or Nietzsche. This is all very nice, but personally, I think Micah is more likely to be the next Jack the Ripper. For those of you who saw the classic movie "Toy Story," he's sort of like Sid, the horrible neighbor child who terrorizes everyone and is a constant source of grief.

When the mother comes over to visit, she naturally brings Micah along with her, and the little wretch causes nothing but trouble, especially for me. The first thing he does when he sees me is to shriek like a banshee and chase me under the bed. Then when I finally come out, he throws my cat toys at me. Naturally, he pulls my tail whenever he can, and when he pets me, it's more like Mike Tyson "petting" Evander Holyfield.

Of course, Micah's mother thinks all this is very cute, and Steve's female, because she is the woman's friend, puts up with it. Steve, on the other hand, has come to my rescue on more than one occasion, only to be harshly told by the mother, "Don't be mean to Micah. He's ONLY a child."

Well, child or not, when Micah torments me, he must pay. The problem is, if I retaliate and lash out at him, or even hiss at him, he starts to cry. Then the mother overreacts and hellfire rains down on me. Talk about injustice. And God forbid I should accidentally scratch the little bugger. The mother would probably take him to the emergency room for treatment and demand that I be charged with assault and battery.

So naturally, I must resort to a bit of cleverness (which some might call sneakiness) to deal with Micah.

When Micah and his mother come over to visit, the mother and Steve's female pay homage to the little horror by gushing over him for five minutes or so. After that, they have coffee while Micah goes and plays by himself in the next room.

This is when I unleash my patented kitty-from-hell treatment.

The first thing I do is enter the room where Micah is playing, sit a safe distance away, and glare at him with my scariest kitty face... that is, I squint my eyes demonically and open my mouth ever so slightly to reveal my evil looking Dracula-like fangs. Sometimes I'll even let out a little unearthly moan just to let Micah know that yes, I am possessed by Satan. If he throws something at me, I use my catlike ability to dodge the object, all the while maintaining my scary demeanor. If he runs out of the room to get his mommy as he often does – the little wuss – I quickly pretend to be asleep, and when they return, I give them a drowsy "I don't know what you're talking about" look. This usually causes the mother to calm Micah by saying something like, "Don't worry. Quasi won't hurt you. He just wants to be with you while you play."

Yeah, right.

When the mother leaves, I'll resume my demonic staring, only this time, I'll take a few ominous steps toward Micah, which really freaks him out. If he tries anything funny, like pulling my tail or something, I'll give him a nice juicy hiss and a couple ferocious whaps (with soft paws, of course... as I said, I don't want to send the little scoundrel to the emergency room). This will cause Micah to once again run out of the room to get his mommy. By the time they return and Micah points an accusatory finger at me, I'll be calmly washing myself or staring complacently out the window like the harmless, cuddly kitty I truly am.

Yeah, right.

Usually, after I've repeated this process five or six times, the mother will become frustrated and take Micah to sit with her and Steve's female. At this point, I'll come strolling out of the next room, give Micah one more evil stare when no one is looking just to let him know who's the boss, and go find a nice peaceful place to sleep.

So, fellow cat, if you're ever besieged by a precocious little human like Micah, just give 'em the 'ole kitty-from-hell treatment. You may have to do it several times, but if you keep it up, you're certain to be victorious.

Still, the simple fact is that children are here to stay, and if it even looks like you're going to cause a child any harm, you'll probably be in for some extreme unpleasantness yourself. So sometimes, as in so many instances when trouble (or scariness) arises, the best thing to do is go somewhere safe and hide out until the storm passes.

Words and Phrases That Are Not in a Cat's Vocabulary

One significant difference between cats and dogs, other than the fact that cats are free spirits and dogs are robotic dummies, is that dogs will always do what humans tell them to do and cats will not (unless they feel like it). For example, if a human says "Stay" to a dog, the dog won't move until the human says it's okay. If a human says "Speak" to a dog, the dog will bark. If a human says "Sit" to a dog, the dog will sit down. If a human says, "Stay," "Speak" or "Sit" to a cat, most likely nothing will happen... unless, of course, the cat is in the mood to stay, meow or sit at the time.

Based on psychological testing and behavioral studies, researchers have determined that there are ten human words and phrases that simply do not exist in a cat's vocabulary. Actually, between us kitties, we know these words and phrases all too well, but unless it suits our pleasure or we happen to feel magnanimous toward our humans at the moment, we most often choose to ignore them.

Here are the ten words and phrases that are not in a cat's vocabulary (wink wink). For some of you foreign kitties who may be reading this, I've included the words in German, French and Spanish (respectively) in addition to English...

NOOOOOO!
Nein!
Non!
Negativa!

STOP!
Halten!
Arreter!
Dejar!

DON'T!
Nicht!
Ne!
Prohibito!

WAIT!
Warten sie!
Attendez!
Espere!

GET DOWN!
Herunterkommen!
Descendre!
Bajar!

QUIET!
Beruhigen!
Tranquilliser!
Hacer callar!

BE PATIENT!
Sich gedulden!
Etre patient!
Ser paciente!

DON'T GO IN THERE!
Gehen nicht drin!
Ne vont pas la-dedans!
No vaya alli!

LET ME SLEEP!
Gestatten sie mir zu schlafen!
Laissez-moi dormir!
Me deja dormir!

IT'S NOT ALL ABOUT YOU!
Es ist nicht alles uber sie!
Ce n'est pas tout sur vous!
No es todo a cerca di ti!

How to Punish Your Human When They Leave You Home Alone

Even though many humans hate to leave their cat (or cats) alone for more than five minutes, there are times when they go on trips for days on end. Some of these trips are known as vacations, where humans go somewhere nice and goof off. This is all fine and dandy for them, but what about us poor, neglected kitties who are left at home alone (the pet sitter doesn't count). This is unacceptable human behavior and must not go unpunished.

Now before you lower the gavel and send your human to the gallows or the guillotine, you must first determine if they did, in fact, go on a vacation. You don't necessarily want to initiate corporal punishment every time your human leaves the house (although you certainly can if you want to). Some humans are pretty sneaky, so it may be a little difficult to figure out what they're up to when they go out the front door. Still, most humans do something to give themselves away when they are preparing for a long trip. All you have to do is look for changes in their normal daily patterns, or the introduction of new objects.

In our house, it's the dreaded black bags. A day or two before Steve and his female go on a trip, these bags, also known as suitcases, appear on the floor of the bedroom. If just one of the smaller bags is brought out, that usually means it's only Steve who's leaving. If just one small and one medium-size bag are brought out, that usually means it's only the female who's leaving. But if all the bags are brought out, including the big square-shaped one, that means they're both going.

When I've determined for certain that Steve and the female are going on a trip, I begin the punishing process immediately by making them feel guilty. That is, I poke around the suitcases, all the while looking up at them with my pleading kitty eyes as if to say, "You're not really leaving me, are you?" I always throw in a few plaintive meows just to make sure they get the message and feel super guilty. And, for good measure if one of the suitcases is left open, I'll crawl in and get kitty hair all over their neatly-packed clothing. Now that Bo Diddley and Piglet have joined our household, we can triple team Steve and his female and compound the guilt. You see, fellow forsaken kitty, guilt is a very important aspect of teaching your human a lesson for leaving you. The point is, when they're lying on some sunny beach somewhere or prowling the streets of *Par-ee*, you want them to think about you at home and experience crushing, vacation-ruining guilt.

Next, you want to determine the level of damage to inflict within the household to teach your human a lesson for abandoning you at home while they're off having fun. If they are just gone for the weekend, you might want to cut them some slack and only trash a few things such as houseplants. However, if your human is gone for a week or more, you'll want to pull out all the stops and rain down cruel, unrelenting destruction. If total destruction is your game, wait until after your pet sitter's final visit... otherwise, the pet sitter will clean up your mess and negate all your hard work (and make your human think it's okay to go on a vacation anytime they want). This may not leave you a lot of time to turn your household into a candidate for aid from FEMA, but if execute your scorched earth policy creatively and quickly, you'll have plenty of time to do you worst and still take a nice, rejuvenating nap afterward.

Here's a list of the teach-them-a-lesson-for-leaving-me damages I typically inflict (with help from B.D. and Pig) when Steve and the female leave us alone for a week or more...

- ❖ 1 unraveled (and microscopically-shredded) roll of toilet paper.

- ❖ 3 wastebaskets knocked over and rummaged through.

- ❖ Contents of wastebaskets strategically strewn around floor.

- ❖ Litter cavalierly flung out of litter box.

- ❖ Über-shredding on arm of couch.

- ❖ 1 kacked-up hairball on coffee table (with fallout spatter on DVD remote).

- ❖ At least 1 lamp knocked over (with the bulb shattered if possible).

- ❖ 4 chewed-up leaves on female's favorite houseplant.

❖ Use of dirt in houseplant for... well, you know.

❖ All cat toys strewn about the house.

❖ At least 1 *objet d'art* knocked over and broken.

❖ All moveable items on female's dressing table ruthlessly batted onto floor.

❖ Teeth marks on Steve's one pair of dress shoes (he never wears them anyway).

❖ Vomitus on at least one pillow on the bed.

❖ All books shoved out of the bookcase and onto the floor (except *The World Is Your Litter Box* of course).

❖ Overall smell of cat throughout house.

❖ Cat hair on everything.

And for the real *coup de gras*, be sure to scorn and shun your human for at least one solid hour after they arrive home before letting them back into your good graces. Doing this will make them feel even more guilty (and lessen the chance that they'll punish you for all the household damage). When Steve and the female came home from their last vacation, they were so grateful when B.D., Pig and I finally relented and turned on the charm that Steve gave us each a handful of treats (this was on top of all the treats we conned our pet sitter into giving us while they were gone). And they cleaned up the mess without complaint. Still, just to let them know I wasn't happy about the whole thing, I gave the large suitcase a fearsome juicy hiss and a couple vicious whaps before it was put away, hopefully for good.

Quasi's Wild Weekend

What with all the normal responsibilities of a cat combined with the added pressure of being a bestselling author, many cats have asked me, "Geez, Quasi, how do you stand the stress? Do you get any time to kick back and relax?"

The answer to that question is yes and no (how's that for sounding like a politician?). The fact is, I can never completely let down my guard or shirk my numerous kitty tasks around the household. As I'm sure you know, a cat's work is never done. And the demands of being an author with unrelenting deadlines, stifling bouts of writer's block, and a public thirsty for MORE, MORE, MORE... well, it's definitely a challenge.

Still, during breaks in the action, I do manage to squeeze in a little "me" time. Here's how I spend a typical weekend...

Saturday: Watch as Piglet wakes Steve and the female at 6:00 a.m... demand breakfast in a loud and repetitively-annoying voice... roil around the kitchen with Pig and B.D. as Steve dishes up our morning repast... eat breakfast... clean myself and lick my chops for ten minutes... use the litter box and create an hellacious stink... clean myself again... look cute... help the female make the bed... NAP... sit in the window and chatter at delicious-looking birds... wrestle with B.D... induce petting... NAP... eat some "crunchies" (known to some cats as kibble)... clean myself... kack up a hairball... look cute... beat up Pig to teach him a lesson for challenging my alpha maleness... sniff some catnip and listen to the Dave Matthews Band... NAP... go outside and work on my tan (don't worry, I always use sunscreen)...clean myself... go up on the roof and pretend I can't get down, providing major annoyance to Steve and major yuks for me... look cute... NAP... investigate the inside of a new paper bag... work on my plan for world peace.... NAP... go back outside and patrol the yard... stare unblinkingly into a gopher hole for 20 minutes... go back inside and have a good scratch on the arm of the couch... NAP... help Steve restring his guitar... give Pig a few "who's your daddy" whaps to the skull... eat more crunchies... clean myself... NAP... groom the female's hair... bat a toy mouse around until it goes under the refrigerator... NAP... look cute... induce more petting... wrestle with B.D... nibble on a house plant... stand guard duty at the front door... NAP... roil around the kitchen with Pig and B.D. while Steve dishes up our evening meal... eat dinner... clean myself... look cute... NAP... sit in Steve's lap, watch TV and induce more petting... NAP... sit in the female's lap, watch TV and induce more petting... NAP... eat some more crunchies... clean myself... check the house for intruders and evil spirits... jump up on the bed with Pig and B.D. and settle in for a good night's sleep.

Sunday: Watch as Pig wakes Steve and the female at 6:30 a.m. (we generously let them sleep an extra half-hour on Sunday)... demand breakfast in a loud and repetitively-annoying voice... roil around the kitchen with Pig and B.D. as Steve dishes up our morning meal... eat breakfast... clean myself and lick my chops for ten minutes... use the litter box and, well, you know... clean myself again... NAP... help the female wash her hair (she doesn't make the bed on Sunday)... chase Pig and "tree" him at the top of our scratching post (which we never use)... help Steve do the Sunday New York Times crossword puzzle... NAP... stand morning guard duty at the front door... clean myself... calculate the density of the universe... wrestle with B.D... look cute... induce petting... NAP... eat some crunchies... clean myself... go outside and count the clouds passing overhead... watch a game on TV with Steve... NAP... wrestle with B.D. some more.... kack up a hairball... practice innovative new ways of looking cute... have a rousing game of kitty soccer with Pig and B.D. (and a toy mouse)... NAP... induce more petting... give the female a facial with my sandpaper tongue... sniff some catnip with Pig and B.D., then hold paws and sing "Kumbaya"...

NAP... go back outside and chase butterflies... hide under a bush for a couple hours... NAP... go back inside and eat some crunchies... allow Steve to rub my tummy... look cute and contrite after I grab his arm with my claws... NAP... help Steve and the female read more of the Sunday paper... sit in the middle of the living room floor and meditate for 15 minutes... NAP... alert Steve and the female to the sound of a satellite passing overhead... roil around the kitchen with Pig and B.D. while Steve dishes up our dinner... eat dinner... clean myself... NAP... induce more petting... watch TV with Steve and the female and get high-quality lap time from both of them... look cute... induce lots of petting... NAP... hang out with Pig and B.D and discuss our plans for the week ahead... have some nighttime crunchies... clean myself....race around the house and tire myself out... jump up on the bed with Pig and B.D. and settle in for a good night's sleep.

Whew!

Flummoxing Enigmas for Cats

Even though cats are masters of all that is known and unknown and are aware of pretty much everything that goes on around them, there are still some things that are completely perplexing to the kitty mind. Admittedly, it sometimes doesn't take much to flabbergast a cat, but still... there are things that make you blink your eyes in amazement and say "WTF?" Bewildering things that defy all reasonable bounds of logic (from the feline perspective, anyway). Mystifying things beyond all mortal kitty comprehension that cause even the clearest-thinking cat to lock up and become completely flummoxed.

Daylight Savings Time: Here's one that even humans find to be a cause of consternation and falls into the category of "Why do they do it to themselves?" In order to save energy or whatever, humans have come up with something called daylight savings time, which requires them to set their clocks forward one hour in the spring and back one hour in the fall. This is especially inconvenient in the modern age, when most households have at least 86 devices with digital clocks that are highly complicated to reset. Anyway, in the spring, as a result of this ill-conceived idea, 7:00 a.m. becomes 8:00 a.m., and in the fall, 7:00 a.m. becomes 6:00 a.m. I know, it's totally confusing. It bollixes up natural sleep patterns, and for the two or three days it takes to adjust to the time change, everyone is inordinately cranky (me included). Unfortunately for humans, our internal kitty clocks are not quite so easily resettable. Therefore, in the spring, we wake our humans one hour later, and in the fall, we wake them one hour earlier. Hey, if humans wouldn't monkey around with the natural order of things, none of this would happen, so they have only themselves to blame.

Molecular Changes: Despite my extensive knowledge of science, here's something I find completely baffling. Each morning, Steve makes oatmeal, which looks disgusting, but is supposed to be good for you. He starts by boiling water in a pot on the stove and then pouring in the oats, which at this point, are in the form of flakes. After a short period, the water and the oats begin churning and roiling. How do I know this? Because Steve always lifts me up for a look, and as many times as he has done this, I still can't figure out what the hay is going on. After a few minutes, the flakey oats and boiling water somehow merge together and form a gluey type of glop, which Steve then dumps into a bowl and eats. How does it happen? Clearly some type of chemical change is involved, but how oat flakes can turn into a mushy, edible substance (revolting as it may be) is completely mystifying.

Another highly bewildering molecular change involves water... yes, that's right, the clear liquid in the bowl next to your food. Humans take water like this and put it in the freezer part of the refrigerator, and *viola*... the next thing you know, the water has turned into hard, chunky ice. I know that ice has its human uses, but personally, I don't get it. When water is turned into ice, it becomes undrinkable and ridiculously cold – in other words, completely useless to a cat. And how about this for a mindblower... in some parts of the world, where it gets really cold outside, entire lakes and rivers freeze. Humans then walk and skate on this frozen water, and in some places, they even drive on it. This is something a cat would NEVER do. Don't humans realize what would happen if the ice suddenly became soft again?

Too Much Information at Once: Back in the early days of digital technology, when computer operating systems were slow and clunky, computers would crash if humans tried to open too many windows at the same time. Well, the same thing happens to us cats if too much information comes at us all at once. For example, let's say you're playing with a toy mouse and concentrating on biting its little head off, when suddenly, you hear a noise from outside. Then while you're processing that new information, your human calls out your name for some reason. Then a shadow from a passing airplane catches your eye. Then you hear a dog begin to bark. Then an interesting-looking bird appears outside the window. Then you hear the sound of a pop top can opening in the kitchen. Then... uuhhhh. Next thing you know, your sizzling kitty brain is overloaded and you have no choice but to take a long nap and reboot.

Movement of Sunbeams: Let's say you're ready to take a richly-deserved nap and you've found the perfect sunbeam to lie in. You plop yourself down and head off to kitty dreamland. Next thing you know, you feel a slight chill. You wake up and realize that your carefully-selected sunbeam has moved over a few inches. Harrumph, you say as you rouse yourself, move back into the beam, resettle yourself and go back to sleep. Then a few moments later, darned if you don't feel a slight chill again. You wake up to discover that once again, your beam has moved over. I know, fellow cat, it messes with your head. Is this some kind of cruel trick, you wonder? Are the Gods angry at me? Are space aliens subjecting me to sleep deprivation as some kind of experiment? Whatever the reason, it's very perplexing (and highly inconvenient).

Furniture Rearrangement: Every once in awhile, Steve's female will decide that she's tired of the way the furniture is positioned in the living room and forces Steve to shove things around until she finds a suitable new arrangement. This is all fine and good for them, but don't they realize how much this screws things up for me? It's wildly disorienting and thoroughly disruptive. First, I have to recalibrate my in-house flight patterns so I don't knock anything over when I'm bolting around. Then I have to figure out the new tangent plane relationships between the couch and the TV. Then I have to find new favorite places, since many of the old ones are now covered by furniture. Then I have to go around and painstakingly re-scent everything. Talk about exasperating!

Changes In General: Let's face it... we cats tend to like things just the way they are, so anytime a major change occurs in our environment, it completely upsets the proverbial apple cart and boggles our little kitty minds, at least momentarily. Some of us may be a little more flexible than others when it comes to changes, but personally, I'm not a big fan of anything that causes undue confusion for a cat. I've heard the saying that the only thing constant in life is change, but I say we leave changes to chameleons, caterpillars and larvae.

Females: Well, tom cats, need I say anything more?

How to Recover from Embarrasing Situations

As the regal and dignified creatures we are, cats simply cannot allow themselves to suffer embarrassment, especially at the hands of our humans. Embarrassing situations are, well... embarrassing. Yet because of our antics and curiosity, we often find ourselves in situations that are not only awkward, but require rescue. How many times have you found yourself locked in a closet or stuck at the top of a screen door with your claws hopelessly affixed and had to howl for your human to save you? Yes, I know... it makes you feel like a dowager empress who has spilled tea all over herself at a party for snobby upper crust socialites.

In Chinese culture, recovering from an embarrassing or discomforting situation is called saving face. I'm sure all you *māos* (that's Chinese for 'cat') know what I'm talking about. For you non-Asian kitties, the concept of face is all about maintaining dignity and prestige regardless of what humiliating event may have occurred. In other words, it's all about landing on your feet, quickly regaining your composure, and not looking like a complete doofus when something inelegant happens to you.

So what do we cats do when we find ourselves in an embarrassing situation? Well, let me tell you a little story about an incident that was mega-embarrassing for your old pal Quasi and how I rectified the situation and saved face.

About a year ago, before Bo Diddley and Piglet came to live with us, a female neighbor had a boyfriend who often brought his German Shepard along when he visited her. The presence of an additional dog in the 'hood was bad enough, but there's more... this dog happened to be missing his front left leg. I don't know what misfortune may have befallen the poor beast, but regardless, he only had three legs. His owner called him Triad, which for you cats with tin ears, refers to a musical chord with three tones. It could have been worse... the hapless creature could have been named Tripod or Trio or something unflattering like that.

Even though Triad was a dreaded dog, I must admit I felt a little sorry for him. Still, being the king of the cats in the neighborhood, I had to protect my street cred and assert my dominance over him. And from the looks of things, it figured to be pretty easy. After all, I thought, how fast can a dog run on just three legs? So one morning, while Triad was dozing on the front step of the female neighbor's house, I sauntered on over and boldly gave him a little swat on the behind. Nothing serious, mind you... just a little warning shot to let him know that he was in kitty country.

Triad instantly woke up. He glared at me, growled in a low menacing rumble, and bared his fearsome lupine teeth. It was a bit unsettling, sure, but I wasn't too worried. Emboldened by the knowledge that I had four legs and Triad only had three, I gave him my patented "Who's your daddy?" kitty smirk. Triad stirred a bit and barked at me in his thunderous voice. Still emboldened (but not stupid), I backed off a few steps and gave him a nice, juicy hiss.

Suddenly, Triad rose up on all three legs. He barked furiously and started toward me. I saw, to my mortification, that he had no trouble standing or walking. Realizing that I had made a fundamental mistake in challenging a dog, three legs or not, I did the smart thing and bolted off. Once I figured I was a safe distance away, I stopped and turned around. You can only imagine my shock when I saw Triad hurling toward me, teeth gnashing and spittle flying, and closing fast. Yikes!

I never ran so fast in my life. Triad was right behind me, his canine incisors clicking ominously, his hot doggie breath warming my fanny like a marshmallow over a campfire. Fortunately, I was nearing the tree next to our house, and just as Triad was about to grab hold of my tail with his frightful chompers, I hurled myself at the tree and clawed my way up. I was safe from Triad's clamping jaws, but he wasn't about to let me come down. He circled the tree, barking and drooling. The horror, the horror!

Steve heard the noise and came out of the house. When he saw that Triad had me treed, he shooed him away (although, much to my chagrin, he was pretty nice about it). Then, because I was too scared to come down by myself, Steve had to climb up the tree and get me.

As you can image, this little episode was way into the red on the Embarrassment-O-Meter. Being chased up a tree by a three-legged dog was bad enough, but then needing Steve to have to come and rescue me...you can only imagine my shame and humiliation. Talk about losing face.

In embarrassing situations like this, you can do one of two things, or a combination of both if necessary. If the cause of the embarrassment is not too serious, such as getting yourself locked in a closet, you can simply look nonplussed and give your human a "What?" look when they come to rescue you. In other words, be in total denial, or at least give your human the impression that you're so unbelievably cool, you're above being embarrassed. Then strut away with your tail in the air and act like whatever happened was no big deal.

However, in embarrassing situations like the three-legged dog incident where scariness is involved, you'll probably want to play the "fear" card... that is, turn to mush, meow pathetically, and act like you've been permanently traumatized, or at the very least, grievously upset. You might even want to tremble a bit for extra effect. Even if you're not really that scared, act like you are. This will cause your human to feel sorry for you, and instead of thinking that the incident was whimsical or funny, they'll fawn all over you and do whatever it takes to make you feel better. After the three-legged dog incident, Steve cuddled me protectively and dished out lots of extra loving, and because I was so "traumatized," he gave me a nice big handful of treats.

So remember these simple actions the next time you find yourself in an embarrassing situation, especially something harrowing where you must rely on your human to rescue you. The point is, fellow humiliated cat, you don't want your human to laugh at you or tease you about what happened... or worse yet, sell the story to a scandal rag.

And one other piece of advice while I'm handing it out... don't swat at, or otherwise tamper with, three-legged dogs.

How to Comfort Sick (Or Sad) Humans

As a seasoned cat, I'm fully aware that some humans think we felines are cool and aloof and don't care about anyone or anything but ourselves. NOT TRUE. Cats are kind, caring, sensitive creatures, and hard to believe as it may seem, there may be occasions when circumstances require us to put our own needs and desires on the back burner and place our human's interests first.

Now right about here, you're probably thinking, "Put my human's interests before my own pressing kitty needs? Has Quasi lost his bleeding mind?" Well, fellow cat, the truth is that humans live in an extremely complicated hustle-bustle world fraught with problems and difficulties that we cats can hardly imagine. The human world can be unfair and unjust, and all too often, good people get hurt while bad people prosper. Some humans struggle from day to day to earn enough money just to survive. Some humans are constantly frustrated by their station in life and their relationships with other humans. Some humans are so busy racing around that they never stop to appreciate the good things they have. Some humans think the world is going to hell in a hand basket and that there's no hope. And although there are some six billion people on the planet these days, some humans feel isolated and alone. Sadly to say, some humans find themselves in situations where the love of a cat is the only real solace they can count on.

In times of need and distress, as a number of studies have shown, cats provide comfort to humans of all ages, including those who may be elderly or infirm. Cats are also known to have a calming effect on humans who are lonely, depressed, upset, agitated... or just flat-out crazy. The mere act of petting a cat can lower a human's blood pressure, regardless of how amped up or upset they may be. Pretty much all humans unwind and become more relaxed in the wonderful and welcoming presence of a cat. After all, how bad can things really be when you've got a warm, purring bundle of kitty on your lap?

Cats, too, are non-judgmental and give unconditional love regardless of who our humans are or what they may have done. Piglet, for example, is so non-judgmental that if Hitler rose from the dead and came to our house for a visit, Pig would welcome him with bright eyes and open paws and say something like, "Oh, hello Mr. Hitler – *purr purr purr* – so nice to see you – *purr purr purr* – please come in and pet me – *purr purr purr* – and give me some treats – *purr purr, purr.*" Your human may be as saintly as Mother Theresa or as twisted as Hannibal Lechter, but the reality is, when they come home, you really don't care if they spent the day selflessly treating lepers or if they just drove a busload of orphans over a cliff. As long as they are kind to you and keep dishing out the attention and affection (and food), they will always be worthy of your love with no strings attached.

If your human is like most other humans, you will find that from time to time, they'll need your unabashed, unconditional kitty love to make them feel better and round off the rough edges of life. And when they do, as I said earlier, you must put your own wants and desires aside and soothe them as only a cat can.

Fortunately, it's so ridiculously easy for a cat to comfort a sick or a sad human that it requires practically no effort at all. In fact, it's so easy, you can even take a nap while you're doing it. And as an added bonus, the process of consoling your human will provide you with some very pleasant side benefits. It's a win-win situation for all.

Let's say your human is feeling sick or sad about something, and is sitting in a chair. Jump up in their lap, look into their eyes with love, and softly meow a couple times as if to say, "There, there... everything will be alright." Then settle down and begin purring immediately. This will cause your human to pet you, and the warm, calming feel of your fur, plus the gentle rumbling of your purring will immediately begin to make them feel better. Let your human continue to pet you and tell you their troubles if they want to. Be a good listener even if you have no idea what they're talking about, and be sure to keep up the purring. Don't be in a hurry to rush off... like I said, you can even take a little nap if you like. The point is you want to be there for your human and let them know that no matter what might be going on in their life, you're in their corner.

If your human is in bed and not feeling well, stroll into the bedroom and announce your presence with a couple sweet, friendly meows. Jump up on the bed, start purring, and march around a bit. This will cause your human to smile and reach out to pet you. Nestle right in next to your human with your back toward them and your tummy exposed and keep up the purring. This will cause your human to hold you close (spooning, I believe it's called) and rub your tummy. And for God's sake, hard as it may be, don't grab and bite their arm. The warmth of your furry kitty body and your comforting purr will be the only antidote your human will need to feel better... unless they're really, really ill and need to take some type of distasteful medicine prescribed by their doctor (the human version of the vet).

There may be occasions, though, when your human is awash in sadness and practically inconsolable. Maybe they lost a loved one or received some especially bad news about something. Times like these may require extra kitty love and sympathy, so in addition to spending quality lap or bed time with your human and purring as they pet you, reach out a caring and understanding paw and place it gently on top of your human's hand or whatever part of their body might be handy. You can even touch their face if you want. Move your claws lightly in and out in a soft, caressing manner, all the while purring and meowing tenderly. Even the gloomiest human won't be able to resist a smile.

And then, for the final *acte d'amour*, rise up on all fours, get up close to your human's face and repeatedly rub your head against their chin... that's right, a flurry of kitty kisses to let them know that no matter what, in your eyes, they're the greatest human in the world.

Yes, fellow consoler, the human world can be a very scary place at times... sort of like a vacuum cleaner that never shuts off, a perpetual trip to the vet, or a dog that never stops chasing you. But the simple, inescapable fact is that kitty love can conquer all. If someone could somehow figure out how to bottle a cat's love and affection and hand it out to every human on Earth, the world would be a much better (and calmer) place.

Quasi's Quiz for Cats #2

Can you believe it, fellow cat? Just when you thought your overloaded kitty brain couldn't possibly hold any more data, you've actually managed to cram in the all the information in *The World Is STILL Your Litter Box*. But will you actually remember any of this stuff once you close the book and move on to other things, such as patrolling the yard or supervising your human's activities? You certainly don't want this valuable knowledge to go to waste, so to make sure you retain everything, take the following quiz (and no coaching from your human).

1. To determine whether your human is a true cat nut, you should:
   A. Ask if they like you more than *American Idol*.
   B. Make them take a lie detector test.
   C. Call them a cat nut poseur and watch their reaction.
   D. Commit an act of unacceptable kitty behavior and see if you can get away with it.

2.   Your human is a true cat nut if they allow you to:
   A.   Take up the whole bed at night
   B.   Leave your cat toys strewn around the house.
   C.   Shred the arm of the couch.
   D.   All of the above.

3.   When living with multiple cats, you should:
   A.   Spread vicious rumors about your co-kitties.
   B.   Break something and blame it on one of the other cats.
   C.   Tell your co-kitties that your human likes you best.
   D.   Determine your place in the pecking order.

4.   When pitting your cuteness against other cats in the household, you should:
   A.   Strut your stuff like a bantam rooster.
   B.   Wear provocative clothing.
   C.   Pout and preen like a supermodel.
   D.   Have your best cute kitty pose at the ready

5.   If you're the alpha male and another cat challenges you, you should:
   A.   Squint your eyes and say, "I'm the sheriff in this town."
   B.   Give 'em a taste of your "swagga."
   C.   Turn the other cheek (yeah, right!)
   D.   Hiss and moan and unleash a flurry of whaps.

6. Some fun things to do with the other cats in your household are:
   A. Watch shows about lions and tigers on Animal Planet.
   B. Play Tetris.
   C. Have profound, scholarly dinner conversations.
   D. Engage in cooperative destruction.

7. When preparing for a fight with another cat, you should:
   A. Put up your dukes (or, in this case, your paws).
   B. Tell your opponent they look like a "puss."
   C. Bribe the referee before the fight.
   D. Assume the attitude of a fighting machine.

8. Some good fighting techniques are:
   E. Distract and pounce.
   F. Death from above.
   G. Tummy decoy.
   H. All of the above.

9. Some good defensive techniques are:
   A. The rear-legged defense.
   B. The four-legged defense.
   C. The 180-degree roll.
   D. All of the above.

10. (Bonus Question) The greatest works of literature known to mankind are:
    A. *War and Peace.*
    B. *Gone with the Wind.*
    C. *The Iliad.*
    D. *The World Is Your Litter Box and The World Is STILL Your Litter Box.*

11. To annoy your human just for fun, you should:
    A. Play your music really, really loud.
    B. Eat the leftovers they were saving for dinner.
    C. Push them to the brink of insanity.
    D. Get in their way when they're trying to do something.

12. Other Ways to Annoy your human just for fun are:
    A. Chatter incessantly while they're watching TV.
    B. Invite hooligans over to play.
    C. Stay out late.
    D. Give the arm of the couch a quick shred and gleefully bolt away.

13. You should use a breezy excuse for unacceptable kitty behavior when:
    A. You're feeling flip and sassy
    B. You don't feel witty enough to come up with a clever retort.
    C. You're called to testify before a Congressional committee.
    D. You don't have time to think up a more detailed excuse.

14. If you have to babysit guest kittens, you should:
    A. Try and remain calm.
    B. Tell the kittens scary bedtime stories that will freak them out.
    C. Make sure you know where plenty of duct tape is located.
    D. Teach the kittens the fine art of wreaking havoc.

15. If you're babysitting guest kittens and they pester you, you should:
    A. Spank their fluffy little kitty behinds.
    B. Bat them around like pinballs.
    C. Tell them you're not a doctor and you don't have patience.
    D. Try to ignore them and hope they go away soon.

16. Fun things to do when you're buzzed on catnip are:
    A. Stare out the window... for hours and hours and hours.
    B. Tell everyone in the neighborhood how groovy you feel.
    C. Visualize Google Earth views of Pittsburgh.
    D. Stand on your hind legs and play air guitar.

17. When you're buzzed on catnip, you should not:
    A. Volunteer for dangerous missions.
    B. Dwell on the cruel injustices of life.
    C. Operate a rip saw.
    D. Fall asleep in your litter box.

18. If your human puts you on a diet, you should:
    A. Go on "The Biggest Loser."
    B. Tell them your weight is right where you want it to be.
    C. Tell them your "fatness" is an optical illusion.
    D. Make them sorry they came up with such a stupid idea.

19. To get food when you're on a diet, you should:
    A. Grovel and plead like a pathetic, hungry wretch.
    B. Act like you're dying of starvation.
    C. Threaten to take a bite out of your human's leg.
    D. Find a cat-loving neighbor and con them into feeding you.

20. Cats are way smarter than humans because:
    A. They know that when a tree falls in a forest, it DOES make a sound.
    B. They know the atomic weight of all the elements.
    C. They've figured out how to get humans to do their bidding.
    D. They don't smoke cigarettes or drink alcohol.

21. To make sure your human keeps your litter box clean, you should:
    A. Go into your litter box and yell, "Ewwwwww!"
    B. Put on a haz-mat suit before you approach your box.
    C. Report your human to the EPA.
    D. Have an "accident" outside the box.

22. Another way to make sure your human keeps your litter box clean is:
    A. Take a whiff of your litter box and keel over.
    B. Go into your box and holler, "Who died in here?"
    C. Sing, "I Got 'Dem 'Ole Dirty Litter Box Blues Again."
    D. Leave an especially stinky deposit.

23. If an infant joins your household, you should:
   A. Exclaim, "That's the funniest looking cat I've ever seen!"
   B. Challenge them to an upchucking contest.
   C. Jump up into their crib and pretend to suck out their breath.
   D. Make certain you continue to get your fair share of attention.

24. If a precocious little brat is tormenting you, you should:
   A. Ask them if they prefer being bitten or scratched.
   B. Twist their arm and give them an "Indian burn."
   C. Tell them you know exactly where their carotid artery is located.
   D. Give them the "kitty-from-hell" treatment.

25. To punish your human when they go on a vacation and leave you home alone, you should:
   A. Call and report their Visa card stolen.
   B. Change the lock on the front door.
   C. Run up their heating and electric bills.
   D. Inflict teach-them-a-lesson-for-leaving-me damages.

26. Some enigmas that flummox cats are:
   A. Daylight savings time.
   B. Molecular changes.
   C. Females.
   D. All of the above.

27. On the weekend, the most enjoyable thing for a cat to do is:
    A. Nap.
    B. Nap.
    C. Nap.
    D. Nap.

28. To recover from an embarrassing situation, you should:
    A. Do a quick cartwheel and end with "Ta-da!"
    B. Quickly change the subject.
    C. Put a paw to your face and say, "Oh, dear me!"
    D. Act like the embarrassing situation never happened.

29. To comfort your human when they're sick or sad, you should:
    A. Let them play with your cat toys.
    B. Call a 24-hour moratorium on kitty antics.
    C. Tell them to "suck it up."
    D. Cuddle with them and purr.

30. Cats are the coolest animals on Earth because:
    A. They have overwhelming cuteness.
    B. They like rockabilly music.
    C. They don't act like dogs
    D. They... well, they just are.

Closing Words

As the sun sets in the west, filling the sky with breathtaking mystical colors, I sit on the veranda sipping a cool drink (of water), contemplating my place in the universe and collecting my final thoughts for *The World Is STILL Your Litter Box*. Yes, that's right... searching for words poetic and weighty in import that will not only serve as a fitting conclusion to my second book, but will take their place in the annals of great literature to be read by generations of cats (and cat lovers) in the imponderable future.

Actually, what I'm really doing is sitting on the back of the couch behind Steve as we try and come up with a clever way to put this sucker to bed. The fact is you don't want to just dash off some drivel merely to fill a couple pages and tie a pretty bow on the package. No, a true author (like me) wants to leave their dear readers (like you) with substantive and meaningful words that will linger long after the book has been placed back on the shelf. It's not easy, believe me. I'm sure James Joyce went through the same thing when he was putting the crowning touches on *Ulysses* (or maybe not).

Anyway, fellow cat, let me begin by saying that I hope you enjoyed *The World Is STILL Your Litter Box* as much as I enjoyed writing it and Steve enjoyed typing it. I also hope the book was a richly rewarding read that has enhanced your life, elevated your consciousness to another plane, and provided some good laughs along the way.

Now, having said that, I want you to go out and tell all your cat loving friends to buy copies for themselves and their cat loving friends. All this talk about fine literature is very nice, but we need to sell some books here! Cat food isn't getting any cheaper these days, and now that I'm part of a three-kitty family, we need to keep the cash flowing in (and our tummies full).

Seriously, though, I want to thank each and every human who has provided a good and loving home for a cat, and in many instances, multiple cats. You truly are, without a doubt, the best humans on earth. Thanks also to the veterinarians of the world for taking such good care of us (even though going to the vet is STILL one of my least favorite things). Thanks to the extraordinary animal rights organizations and rescue groups that work so hard to make sure all animals – yes even dogs – are properly cared for and treated with kindness. Thanks to whoever discovered catnip and its wonderful, mindbending effect on us felines. And lastly, thanks to the cat food manufacturers for making entrails, gristle and unspeakable offal taste so darn good.

And me? Well, now that this book is done, I can get back to my normal routine of napping 20 hours a day while using the remaining time for such important tasks as eating, grooming and looking cute. Of course, I'm always available for personal appearances and guest spots on TV talk shows (Oprah? Dave? The View?), and I'm always ready to lend a paw to further the cause of kitties everywhere. And before I go, if you'll allow me just one last indulgence, I want to send a big meow out to Steve and his female. Hey guys, even though I may not show it at times (I am a cat, after all), you mean the world to me and I love you.

So finally, in closing... hey what's this I see? Is that Piglet getting ready to make yet another assault on my alpha maleness? Yes, I believe it is. I guess I'll just have to leave my final words for another time, because right now, it's time for me to right the ship, restore order and kick some kitty butt!

Your best kitty friend forever,

Breinigsville, PA USA
14 July 2010
241761BV00001B/10/P